TAKING BACK THE GOSPEL

BAILEY SMITH

HARVEST HOUSE PUBLISHERS
Eugene, Oregon 97402

Cover by Left Coast Design, Portland, Oregon

TAKING BACK THE GOSPEL

Copyright © 1999 by Bailey Smith
Published by Harvest House Publishers
Eugene, Oregon 97402

Library of Congress Cataloging-in-Publication Data

Smith, Bailey. E.
    Taking back the gospel / Bailey Smith.
        p. cm.
    Includes bibliographical references.
    ISBN 0-7369-0065-9
    1. Christian life—Baptist authors. I. Title.
BV4501.2.S525 1999
230'.044'0973—dc21

                                    98-45765
                                      CIP

99 00 01 02 03 04 / BC / 10 9 8 7 6 5 4 3 2 1

This book is affectionately dedicated to my pastor, Dr. Johnny Hunt, a passionate preacher, a loving pastor, an exciting Christian, and a cherished friend. And also to his loving wife Janet, a precious example of Christian grace.

I further dedicate *Taking Back the Gospel* to my fellow church members at the First Baptist Church of Woodstock, Georgia, who love to share the gospel of our Lord Jesus Christ.

Acknowledgment

I am grateful to Joe Johnson of Nashville, Tennessee, a former editor with a major publisher and a great preacher of the gospel. His insight, advice, and willingness to listen and respond were extremely helpful in the completion on this work. Thank you, dear friend.

Contents

The Reshaping of Christianity. 7

1. A Cross Without Blood. 9

2. A Salvation Without a Lord. 23

3. A Hell Without Reality 39

4. A People Without Purity. 57

5. A Church Without Compassion. 75

6. A Bible Without Trust. 89

7. A Christ Without Distinction 103

8. A Worship Without Spirit 117

9. A Church Member Without Conversion. 127

10. A Preacher Without Power 143

11. A Society Without a Conscience 163

12. A Ministry Without Urgency. 175

Notes. 193

MATT, 26,28
"Nothing BuT The Blood OF Jesus"

The Reshaping of Christianity

The gospel of Jesus Christ has always been the heart and core of Christianity. The apostle Paul said: "I am not ashamed of the gospel of Christ; for it is the power of God unto salvation" (Romans 1:16). For 20 centuries, believers have risked their lives to proclaim the gospel to the world. Hearts have been convicted, souls converted, and lives changed. The simple gospel of the grace of God in Christ Jesus has triumphed time and time again.

Yet as we enter the twenty-first century, voices are suggesting that we need to make the gospel more "user-friendly." Dumbing down the message and lightening up the requirements will gain us a better hearing, we are often told. After all, this is the age of lite foods and beverages. Why not a lite gospel?

In Christian circles, this trend comes across as an attempt to make the gospel more appealing to the unchurched. It involves a watering down of the essential ingredients of the true gospel. This new gospel lite eliminates the unpleasantries of repentance, conviction, commitment, and true conversion. It allows the sinner to come to Christ without relinquishing his sin. It opens the fellowship of the church to those who show no intention of submission to the holdings and authority of Christ.

The mainline churches in America have been in decline ever since they embraced this mentality early in the twentieth century. Now, many evangelicals are suggesting the same approach. Accommodation has replaced confrontation.

Truth has been eliminated in favor of consensus. The distinctives of the faith have been replaced by politically correct concerns about human welfare. The Christ of the Bible has been reduced to a fallible humanitarian. Salvation has been repackaged as a process of social redemption. And the gospel has been reshaped into a feel-good experience.

Forgotten in today's "gospel revisionism" is the message that sent Christ to the cross and disciples to martyrdom. Today's gospel lite is hardly worth living for and certainly not worth dying for. It produces a "What's in it for me?" mentality that saps the life out of true Christianity.

The *lite* gospel will never replace the gospel *light*. The truth, and only the truth, sets us free. Jesus calls us to surrender ourselves to Him in complete abdication of our wills to His will. He asks us to take up the cross and follow Him.

This book is a call to all genuine Christians to turn from the lite back to the light. Our generation needs the clear prophetic voice of truth to cut through all our self-centeredness and bring us back to the cross of Jesus Christ. What a tragedy if the true gospel were to be lost in our generation because we tried to lighten the message instead of proclaiming the Light!

Jesus said, "Whosoever shall be ashamed of me and of my words, of him shall the Son of man be ashamed" (Luke 9:26). This is not the time to back down. It is the time to move forward—with the cross of Jesus and the banner of the gospel. May God help us to keep the light shining in our generation!

—Bailey Smith
Atlanta, Georgia

— 1 —

A Cross
Without Blood

*Most important, whenever our own conscience
would mercilessly condemn us, the blood of
Christ cries for forgiveness. Christ's atonement
fully satisfied the demands of God's righteousness, so forgiveness and mercy are guaranteed to
those who receive Christ in humble, repentant
faith. We accept the responsibility for our sin,
and also believe God that in the death of Christ
sin is forgiven. We confess our sin so that the
Lord can cleanse our conscience and give us
joy (1 John 1:9). That is how "the blood of
Christ, who through His eternal Spirit offered
Himself without blemish to God, cleanse[s]
your conscience from dead works to serve the
living God" (Hebrews 9:14). In other words,
our faith communicates to our conscience that we
are pardoned through the precious blood of
Christ.*[1]

—John F. MacArthur

As we rush onward into the twenty-first century, do you
ever feel that the United States is becoming a pagan
nation? Are you chagrined and disappointed because it

seems the majority of Americans not only reject Christ but oftentimes poke fun at evangelical churches and Christian doctrine?

Do you believe that the United States could have been legitimately called "Christian" perhaps four or five decades ago? Do you sense that our civilization has moved away from its Judeo-Christian moral and ethical moorings, often spurred on by so-called multipluralism or multiculturalism, anti-Christian organizations, and a biased liberal press?

We are living in the time of polls, both secular and religious. For the last five years the Barna Research Group, a Christian organization, has conducted a thorough poll concerning religion in the United States. The most recent *Barna Report* noted:

> When God displayed His true character for humankind, through His encounters with the patriarchs of Israel, through handing down the Ten Commandments, and through His promises to Israel through the covenant He formed with His people, He left little ambiguity about who He is. Today, the concept of belief in God remains solid in most people's lives. What is more revealing, though, is how we construe "god." One out of three Americans believes in a conception of God that conflicts with the biblical portrait of the Father.[2]

The *Report* also indicated that

> Most Americans...reject the notion of absolute truth. A growing proportion of people, now up to one-third of the population [does] not believe in the God described

in the Bible, but have other notions of who (or what) God is or means. Most adults do not believe that Satan is a real being. Most people believe that it does not matter what god you pray to because every deity is ultimately the same deity, shrouded in different names and attributes by humankind. A minority of Americans have a personal relationship with Jesus Christ. Nearly two out of three adults contend that the choice of one religious faith over another is irrelevant because all faiths teach the same basic lessons about life. Americans are nearly evenly divided regarding whether or not Christ was perfect; almost half of the public believe that Jesus made mistakes while He was on earth.[3]

Barna continued:

Given the fact that not quite 4 out of 10 adults may be described as born-again believers, it is quite telling to realize that more than 8 out of 10 adults (85%) believe that Jesus was crucified, died and resurrected *and is spiritually alive today*. To recognize that half of all the people who accept the biblical account of Jesus' death, resurrection, and eternal life nevertheless have not sought any type of serious, permanent relationship with Him is rather astonishing. This must raise some questions both about our culture *and the ways the American church fosters its faith within the context of this culture* (emphasis added).[4]

An Unfortunate Reluctance

For those who have actively ministered and witnessed for Christ over several decades, Barna's findings are not surprising. Since almost 50 percent of Americans question Jesus' perfect character, it is understandable they would have difficulty believing in the efficacy of His shed blood on the cross. Self-centered mankind recoils from the concept of Jesus Christ's dying for its sins. Barna's statement "the ways the American church fosters its faith within the context of this culture" is necessarily provocative.

Far too many churches and their ministers—either intellectually and/or spiritually—do not accept Christ's atoning blood. Or, even if they do accept it, they hesitate to proclaim it emphatically. Multitudes of churches acknowledge the doctrine of the substitutionary atonement but are reluctant to preach and teach it. What, then, could we expect from the public at large, who, if it is exposed to preaching at all, often hears a watered-down pep talk that focuses on self-image, self-esteem, and self-love? Today's church is more concerned about the satisfaction of self rather than the sacrifice of self.

Yet consider the indignities and insults genuine believers have borne since the inception of Christianity. A cursory scan of the New Testament reveals ample persecution. *Foxe's Book of Martyrs* lists many deeply moving accounts of people who paid with their lives for their faith. Then there is the world news that is often suppressed—as you read this, millions of believers around the world are suffering persecution, torture, and even death because they love Jesus Christ.

The apostle Paul, the chief proponent of the faith during the first century, lost his head on a Roman chopping block. Read what the pagan, "multicultural" world thought of the gospel he expounded:

> The word of the cross is to those who
> are perishing foolishness [a scandal, an
> inglorious offense], but to us who are being
> saved it is the power of God....For indeed
> Jews ask for signs, and Greeks search for
> wisdom; but we preach Christ crucified, to
> Jews a stumbling block, and to Gentiles
> foolishness, but to those who are the called,
> both Jews and Greeks, Christ the power of
> God and the wisdom of God (1 Corinthians
> 1:18,22-24 NASB).

NO BLOOD—NO SALVATION

For two millennia unregenerate mankind has railed against and ridiculed the Christian doctrine of the atonement: that God dispatched His "only begotten Son," Jesus Christ, into this world for the express purpose of dying on the cross. Unsaved persons, "religious" and nonreligious, are appalled by the cross and precious blood that Christ shed on that cruel instrument of death.

Why did Christ have to die by shedding His blood? So He could become the substitutionary sacrifice for the sins of all human beings before, during, and after His incarnation, even to the end of the world or the consummation of the age.

The cross is what sets Christianity apart from all other religions, cults, and isms of the world. The cross, first of all—and, second, the resurrection. The apostle Paul forcefully declared:

> Moreover, brethren, I declare unto you
> the gospel which I preached unto you,
> which also ye have received, and wherein
> ye stand; by which also ye are saved, if ye
> keep in memory what I preached unto you,
> unless ye have believed in vain.

> For I delivered unto you first of all that which I also received, how that *Christ died for our sins according to the scriptures*; and that he was buried, and that *he rose again the third day according to the Scriptures*: and that he was seen of Cephas, then of the twelve: after that, he was seen of above five hundred brethren at once: of whom the greater part remain unto this present, but some are fallen asleep.
>
> After that, he was seen of James; then of all the apostles. And last of all he was seen of me also, as of one born out of due time (1 Corinthians 15:1-8, emphasis added).

In that passage we find the supreme essence, the strategic entity of the Christian gospel ("the good news," the *euaggelion*): "Christ died for our sins according to the scriptures; and...he was buried, and...he rose again the third day according to the scriptures."

With our finite minds we cannot understand the infinite God, the awesome Creator and Sustainer of the universe who spoke this world, innumerable planets, and stars into existence. Fathom His ways we cannot. In the mind of God the blood of Christ was indispensable, totally essential. Why? Quite frankly, the Bible emphasizes that there is no other way: "without shedding of blood is no remission" (Hebrews 9:22).

The Bible clearly states that Jesus was the Lamb slain before the foundation of the world:

> Ye know that ye were not redeemed with corruptible things, as silver and gold, from your vain conversation received by tradition from your fathers; but with the precious blood of Christ, as of a lamb without

blemish and without spot: who verily was
foreordained before the foundation of the
world, but was manifest in these last times
for you (1 Peter 1:18-20).

The omnipotent, omniscient God—as revealed in the
Bible, God's holy book—realized that man was going to sin.
(Those who normally shy away from the matter of Christ's
blood also prefer to avoid sensitive subjects like sin, or
man's total depravity.) The presupposition for believing in
the blood is an acceptance, first of all, of God's sovereignty,
and second, of His objective revelation, the authoritative
Word of God.

THE SYMBOLISM OF THE CROSS

Many churches display a cross as the centerpiece of
their architecture but recoil at the original idea behind the
cross. Nowadays, the cross is viewed more as an ornament
than a reminder of the high price God paid to reconcile
man to Himself. Even unbelievers wear crosses of various
kinds around their necks or in their earlobes. Years ago so-
called "modernists" began to make light of the blood sacrifice of Christ. They referred to the concept of atonement
as "a religion of the shambles" and "a gospel of gore."
These modernists are still propagating such views to this
day.

Virtually gone is the time when Christians sing songs
like "There Is a Fountain Filled with Blood," "Nothing But
the Blood of Jesus," and "There's Power in the Blood." The
natural tendency is to eschew all mention of the blood for
fear that it will offend. Ironically, many of the same people
who object to any mention of Christ's blood don't give a
second thought to the rampant violence and bloodshed
that appears in today's movies and television shows.

A bloodless cross, however, is no cross at all. So many
have tried to tiptoe around the cruciality of the cross.

Incidentally, the word *cruciality* is derived from the Latin word *crux,* meaning "cross." If the cross merely stands for religion, it is pointless. One can take God's name in vain in more ways than with one's mouth. When a person who indulges in a lifestyle of sin wears a cross and ignores the very reason that Christ shed His blood, he is, in a sense, taking God's name in vain. He is making a mockery of the cross.

The late Loraine Boettner, a conservative Presbyterian scholar, reverently observed:

> It is not enough to recognize Christ as a teacher while rejecting Him as the atoning Saviour. In the conversation with Nicodemus He promptly brushed aside the complimentary words, "We know that thou art a teacher come from God," and declared that until one is born anew he cannot even so much as see the kingdom of God. And similarly the pity of the "Daughters of Jerusalem," although doubtless was sincere, was rejected apparently because it did not represent the fact that His suffering was not for Himself but for others....And the rending of the veil of the temple, which symbolized that the way into the presence of God had been opened for all men, occurred not at His baptism, nor at the Sermon on the Mount, but *at His death* (emphasis added).[5]

CHRIST'S BLOOD: A NECESSARY ELEMENT

So many believers have confessed to me their angst over listening to preaching that deemphasizes the fundamental themes of the Christian faith, including the blood atonement of Christ. Those who have left such preaching have noticed the dramatic difference that results when they place themselves under the teaching of a pastor who proclaims the full counsel of God's Word, including the cross.

Many preachers feel they can walk the so-called fine line of affirming the substitutionary atonement of Christ on the cross without ever touching upon the subject of the blood. Those preachers, some of whom may believe the entire Bible from cover to cover, simply don't want to talk about Christ's bloodshed for fear of scaring away their "sophisticated" congregations.

We may like to think that such compromise will keep a congregation from growing, but that's not the case. It's an exception to the rule, but some of these pastors have growing churches that, unfortunately, are illiterate concerning specific doctrines in God's Word.

There Is No Other Way!

There is only one way of salvation, and that is the way of the blood. Without the shedding of Christ's blood, there would be no forgiveness. As I said in another book,

> A bloodless religion will never transport you to heaven. A bloodless religion will never usher you into the presence of God. A bloodless religion can never settle your sin problem. "What can wash away my sin? Nothing but the blood of Jesus!"[6]

Many people, when they speak about the cross, simply refer to it as a symbol of Jesus' giving His life. Yes, He gave His life, but He did it infinitely more than merely as a good example, a model, or a martyr. Jesus Christ voluntarily offered Himself on behalf of our sins. He died by shedding His blood in order that we would not have to die spiritually to pay the indemnity of our sins against God.

UNDERSTANDING GOD'S LOVE AND JUSTICE

More and more we are hearing people say, "God is so good and loving that He would never send anybody to hell. Neither would He be a bully and have His own Son crucified on a cross, and neither would He allow any of us to be lost. In fact, surely God is going to save everybody."

They are right when they say that God is good and loving, but they are wrong when they say that it's God who sends people to hell. People send *themselves* by rejecting God's offer of forgiveness and salvation through the shed blood of Jesus Christ. If anyone spends eternity in hell, it will be because they did not receive Christ as Lord and Savior. Jesus explained why hell was created:

> Then shall [the King] say also unto them on the left hand, Depart from me, ye cursed, into everlasting fire prepared for the devil and his angels (Matthew 25:41).

Originally, hell was prepared for the devil and his angels, but Satan's adherents, the lost, will follow him directly into eternal torment. In a secondary sense, every follower of the devil is one of his "surrogate angels."

If there were any other means of affording mankind's salvation, God the Father would never have sent Jesus to die on the cross. However, God loved His human creatures so much that He was willing to give up His only begotten Son, who would enter this rebellious world to suffer unspeakably horrible indignity and humiliation.

> Christ Jesus, who, being in the form of God...made himself of no reputation, and took upon Himself the form of a servant, and was made in the likeness of men: And

> being found in fashion as a man, he humbled himself, and became obedient unto death, even the death of the cross (Philippians 2:5-8).

> God so loved the world, that he gave his only begotten Son, that whosoever believeth in him should not perish, but have everlasting life (John 3:16).

> But God commendeth His love toward us, in that while we were yet sinners, Christ died for us (Romans 5:8).

God's desire is for all people to become saved; God is "not willing that any should perish, but that all should come to repentance" (2 Peter 3:9). At the great white throne of judgment, no one will be able to say, "God, You didn't love me. You didn't give me a chance." The Creator of the universe—the God of glory—drained the resources of heaven to provide for the salvation of every man, woman, and child in the entire world, but only a very few are willing to accept His provision.

Yet ours is not only a loving God, but a just God. Man has a sin problem which God cannot ignore with a shrug of the shoulder. Being the righteous God that He is, sin must be punished. And the punishment He decreed was death—eternal separation from Him.

We see both God's love and justice inseparably intertwined in 1 John 2:1-2:

> My little children, these things write I unto you, that ye sin not. And if any man sin, we have an advocate *[trial defense lawyer]* with the Father, Jesus Christ the

righteous; and He is the propitiation *[the substitutionary atonement]* for our sins; and not for ours only, but also for the sins of the whole world.

We may not be able to fully understand how God's love and justice work hand in hand, but we can and must accept the facts as they appear in the Bible.

THE BIG PICTURE

Failing to proclaim the blood of Christ is to breach the commands of our Lord and to neglect the means of our salvation. "Neither is there salvation in any other: for there is none other name under heaven given among men, whereby we must be saved" (Acts 4:12).

It does not bother me for someone to refer to Christ's saving work as "the total event," provided he means that all our Lord did is bound up together and related to His plan of salvation. True, if Jesus had remained on the cross or in the tomb, as Paul expressed it, "we are of all men most miserable" (1 Corinthians 15:19). His incarnation, coming in the flesh, sinless life, miraculous ministry, death, burial, resurrection, ascension, and second coming are all related.

If there had been no incarnation, there would have been no ministry here on earth. If no ministry here on earth, then no teaching and working of signs, wonders, and miracles; if no teaching and working of signs, wonders, and miracles, then no death on the cross; if no death on the cross, then no resurrection; if no resurrection, then no ascension; if no ascension, then no second coming. Without these, there would be no salvation!

> For this is my blood of the new testament, which is shed for many for the remission of sins (Matthew 26:28).

WHY ARE PEOPLE
OFFENDED BY THE BLOOD?

In my book *Nothing But the Blood,* I refer to four basic reasons why people are offended when they hear about Christ's death on the cross.

1. *The cross appears to be defeat when it is actually victory!* How was the cross a victorious event? First, it was because Jesus was not diverted from His purpose. Second, Jesus fulfilled the sacrificial system. Third, Jesus died a kingly death. Fourth, Jesus died willingly. And fifth, Jesus died a complete death.[7]

2. *The cross appears to be the wrong way.* To the world it seemed ridiculous—and still does. In Galatians 5:11 Paul uses the Greek word *skandalon,* which is translated "offense" in the King James Version. The crucifixion and the preaching of it is derided by the unsaved world as a "scandal," an embarrassment, a laughingstock. But it is the opposite from scandalous. Without the cross no human being in history would have a prayer and would have nothing to anticipate but eternity in the bottomless pit.[8]

3. *The cross appears to be death.* It only seems to be death when in actuality it is the embodiment of eternal life for all of those who embrace Jesus Christ by faith.[9]

4. *The cross appears to be the end.* However, it is only the beginning. The cross began a new mission, it began a new manifestation, it began a new ministry, and it began a new might.[10]

CHRIST'S BLOOD: OUR ONLY HOPE

There is no question, then, that we need to make clear the role Christ's blood has in our redemption. To omit Christ's work on the cross is to omit an essential element of the gospel message. Without His blood, there can be no salvation—no hope.

Frank I. Stanton penned these pungent lines:

The rain beat on my window pane;
I said, Come in, O rain, O rain;
Come in out of the dark, deep night,
And wash my soul and make it white.
    But the rain replied,
    For the soul that died
    There is only One, the Crucified.
The wind beat on my window pane,
I said, Come in, O wind, O wind;
Come in out of the wild stormy night
And waft my soul to realms of light.
    But the wind replied,
    For the soul that died
    There is only One, the Crucified.

I.E. Barton added these seven lines:

The blood beat on my window pane,
I said, Come in, O blood, O blood;
The blood came in from Calvary's night,
And washed my soul and made it white.
    And the blood replied,
    For the soul that died,
    I am thine own, the Crucified.

— 2 —

A Salvation Without a Lord

You are a disciple, a learner, a follower of the Christ, whether or not you follow close up. You are a servant of the eternal God, whether you serve well or poorly. You are a soldier in the army of the Lord Jesus Christ, whether you are in the front lines or AWOL. If I know who I am, and if I know who God is, then my so-called rights in life have been subjugated to the Person of God in Jesus Christ—Christos. He is the Lord of my life. And whatever and whenever, I have no cause to bargain with Him or put up an argument. If you and I are purchased possessions of God, Then all that has our names on it belongs to that same God.[1]

—Charles Stanley

More than once, I've heard a person say, "I received Christ as my Savior, but not as my Lord." Sometimes the person will add, "Christ has given me salvation, but I haven't given Him full control of my life."

Because we all know people who profess to be saved but "don't have their act together," we sometimes don't think twice about such statements. In fact, in our day of widespread lack of dedication and commitment among Christians, it may seem that the problem really is just that: Too many people are accepting Christ as Savior, but not as Lord. After all, it's common in today's church to speak of believers who have backslidden or who are indulging in sin yet not doing anything about it. That a person can profess to be a Christian yet not live like one seems to validate the idea that accepting Jesus as Savior and as Lord are two different things.

But is it possible for us to split up the person of Christ in our relationship with Him? Can we separate His role as Savior from His role as Lord?

EXAMINING THE VIEWS

There are some who say that coming to Christ involves no spiritual commitment whatsoever. A person can claim Christ as his own yet display no evidence of change or any willingness to submit to Christ's lordship. That's because salvation is totally apart from works—it's a gift from God, and there's nothing a person can do to earn it. Consequently, we cannot expect good works to be a part of the package. For salvation to be truly free, we are told, it cannot come attached to any conditions.

Greek and New Testament scholar Gerald Cowen describes the proponents of this view in this way:

> On one side of the issue [discipleship and lordship], there are those who separate the gospel message from anything that sounds like a work of righteousness. Their motivation is to keep the gospel pure from the encroachment of human works. The belief of this group is to separate the "objective aspect of Jesus' lordship," recognizing that Jesus is the Lord who rose from the tomb, which is necessary for salvation

and "the subjective sense," which involves making Jesus Lord in a personal sense, which is a part of discipleship. It is possible under this view to be saved without ever making Christ the Lord of one's life....[2]

Now, I firmly agree that salvation is a free gift given totally apart from any good works or requirements on man's part. Scripture is absolutely clear on that truth. I'm not taking issue with that at all. What I *am* questioning is a particular conclusion to which some people have arrived based on that truth. In their endeavor to contend that salvation is a free gift, many sincere authors—including pastors, evangelists, and theologians—have advocated the idea that it's possible for a person to receive Christ as Savior but not Lord. They say submission to Christ's Lordship can come at a later time, if ever at all.

This thinking sort of reminds me of the people who teach that Christians can experience a "second blessing" from God—that accepting Christ is one event, and that you are then to seek a subsequent "baptism in the Holy Ghost." Yet such a view is not supported in Scripture; no one can be saved without the entry and empowering of the Holy Spirit (see John 16: 8-9, Romans 8:9). This old expression articulated by many a saint has stuck with me through the years: "There is one baptism of the Holy Spirit at conversion, but there are many fillings" (see Acts chapter 2 and 4:31).

Getting back to the focal point of this chapter—can we say it's possible for a person to receive Christ as Savior but not Lord? I don't believe so. In fact, I believe that such a teaching is foreign to the New Testament, and you'll see why as we take a careful look at Scripture in the upcoming pages of this chapter.

The Bible itself refers to Jesus as Lord at the very moment a person receives the gift of salvation. Romans 10:9-10, an oft-quoted passage, is a case in point:

> If thou shalt confess with thy mouth the
> *Lord* Jesus [some translations have "confess
> with your mouth Jesus as *Lord*"], and shalt
> believe in thine heart that God hath raised
> him from the dead, thou shalt be saved, for
> with the heart man believeth unto right-
> eousness and with the mouth confession is
> made unto salvation.

In Acts 16:31, one of the Bible's clearest verses about the way to *salvation*, we find Christ's *Lordship* affirmed: "Believe on the *Lord* Jesus Christ, and thou shalt be *saved*." It's important to note that in both verses, Christ's Lordship is assumed. In other words, He is already Lord whether or not we choose to make Him Lord.

Going back to Romans 10:9-10, theologian Gerald Cowen says:

> The confession in Romans 10 implies as
> much that Jesus is my Lord as that He is the
> Lord. When people are freed from sin, they
> become a slave to Christ (Romans 6:14-22).
> ...There is no interim period between
> being saved and becoming a disciple....
> Finally, that is not to say that people
> ever become perfect disciples any more
> than they can have perfect faith, either at
> the beginning or at any other point in the
> Christian life. But, they can be a beginner or
> a mature disciple depending on the progress
> of their growth in Christ. Confessing that
> Jesus is Lord means not only that person's
> acknowledgment that He is God, but that
> they intend to receive Him, however imper-
> fectly, as Master. The answer to the ques-
> tion—Can individuals be saved without ever

receiving Jesus as the Lord of their lives?—is no![3]

What's in a Title?

In reference to the term "Lord," W. O. Carver explained,

> This English word in our Bible represents one Aramaic, three Greek, and nine Hebrew words, two of them in two forms. It thus expresses all grades of dignity, honor, and majesty....It represents the most sacred Hebrew name of God, as their covenant God, *Yah, Yahweh,* and the more usual designation of Deity, *adhonay, Adhon [adonai],* a term which they adopted to avoid pronouncing the most holy designation....[4]

What does one do when he exercises saving faith in Christ as Savior? He also yields himself to Him as Lord. Theologian Walter Thomas Conner affirmed this indisputable truth when he said,

> In the same act in which we receive Him as Savior, we give ourselves to Him as Lord. We become His servants by the virtue of the fact that He saves us from sin.... Therefore, if a man would know God, he must enter the school of Christ, take His yoke, submit to His authority, have the spirit of meekness after The supreme example of Jesus Himself.... So we see that even in the Synoptic Gospels [Matthew, Mark, and Luke] Jesus presents Himself as absolute Lord of conscience and of life, calling for self-surrender on our part....In John's Gospel we find the same truth....

Whichever construction is put upon it, it is sure that Christian faith has at its heart submission to Christ as Lord.[5]

Lord *in the Old Testament*

The use of "Lord" (*adonai*) as synonymous with God takes place repeatedly in the Old Testament. Examples include:

Who may ascend into the hill of the LORD? Any who may stand in His holy place? He who has clean hands and a pure heart, who has not lifted up his soul to falsehood, and who has not sworn deceitfully (Psalm 24: 3-4 NASB).

The LORD is near to all who call upon Him, to all who call upon Him in truth (Psalm 145:18 NASB).

The rich and the poor have a common bond. The LORD is the maker of them all (Proverbs 22:2 NASB).

I, the LORD, am the maker of all things, stretching out the heavens by Myself, and spreading out the earth all alone (Isaiah 44:24 NASB).

Lord *in the New Testament*

The New Testament is rich in its rendering of the word "Lord." The Greek word is *kurios* (sometimes *kurie*), which means "a lord, a master" (see Matthew 12:8); "an owner, possessor" (see Matthew 13:27; Acts 9:6).[6]

All of the foregoing implies the title of Jesus as "Lord." He is our Master, our Owner, our Possessor, our Potentate, our Sovereign, our Power, our Deity. He is nothing less than our *Lord!* Indeed, Jesus is the "King of kings and Lord of lords" (Revelation 19:16). He is....

- the "Lord Christ" (Romans 16:18; Colossians 3:24)
- the "Lord God, the Almighty" (Revelation 15:3)
- the "Lord Jesus" (Acts 7:59; 16:31; Colossians 3:17; 1 Thessalonians 4:2)
- the "Lord Jesus Christ" (Acts 11:17; 20:21; Romans 5:1)
- the "Lord and Savior Jesus Christ" (2 Peter 1:11, 3:18)
- "Lord of all" (Acts 10:36)
- "Lord both of the dead and of the living" (Romans 14:9)
- "Lord of glory" (1 Corinthians 2:8)
- "Lord our righteousness" (Jeremiah 23:6; 33:16)
- "Lord, your Redeemer" (Isaiah 43:14)

Elsewhere in the New Testament we read:

> Yet for us there is but one God, the Father, from whom are all things, and we exist for Him; and one Lord, Jesus Christ, by whom are all things, and we exist through Him (1 Corinthians 8:6).

> And that every tongue should confess that Jesus Christ is Lord, to the glory of the Father (Philippians 2:11).

The title "Lord" is not only a term of respect for Jesus, but repeatedly exalts Him as supreme Lord, Master, King, and Ruler. In the apostle Paul's 13 New Testament epistles, he employed "Lord" in reference to Jesus more than 200 times. Sometimes the title is used by itself or with other words—"the Lord Jesus," "the Lord Jesus Christ," "Jesus Christ our Lord," and "Christ Jesus our Lord."

For a genuinely saved person, then, the Lordship of Christ is not optional. It "comes with the territory." Jesus is Lord and Savior. Those who claim, "I have Jesus as my Savior but not as my Lord" have placed a question mark over their profession of faith. What did "doubting Thomas" cry out when he was confronted with the risen Christ? "My Lord and my God!" (John 20:28). When a person truly recognizes Jesus as his risen Savior, his heartfelt response is, "Jesus, You are my Lord!"

THE COST OF CONFESSING JESUS AS LORD

As far as the first-century Christians were concerned, the worst possible use of "lord" was in the cultic worship of the Roman emperors. When an emperor died, no matter how vicious and hated he was, he was officially exalted to the position of a god in the Roman pantheon. Nero (A.D. 54-68) was probably the first emperor who insisted that his subjects worship him as a god. "Caesar is lord" became a greeting, even as "Heil Hitler" did during the heyday of Nazi Germany. During the reigns of Nero and especially Domitian and Trajan, every loyal Roman subject was supposed to acknowledge that Caesar was lord. In a human sense he was, for he had the power of life and death over untold millions of his subjects.

During the latter quarter of the first century, emperor worship tested the loyalty of every Roman citizen and slave. Once a year, every person was called to burn incense and publicly confess that "Caesar is lord." This practice became so legalistic that every person who carried it out was presented with official credentials stating that he or she had worshiped at the altar of the Caesar-god. Any person who refused to do this was judged guilty of "blaspheming" or speaking evil of Caesar. That, of course, was the final charge leveled against the apostle Paul, for which he was finally beheaded in Rome.

Unspeakably horrible imprisonment, torture, and death awaited those who refused to pledge their allegiance to Caesar as "lord." Stalwart Christians absolutely would not cow down to that custom. Thousands were crucified, hideously tortured to death, burned at the stake, and torn apart by wild beasts in arenas filled with chortling, bloodthirsty mobs. They were bludgeoned to death, drawn and quartered, hacked to pieces, and even used as human torches to light up the gardens of government authorities.

Polycarp, the bishop of Smyrna, was martyred in the mid-second century. His harrowing trial and execution paralleled the deaths of Christians in the first century. Eusebius Pamphylus, an early church historian, related the tragic martyrdom of Polycarp, then 86 years old. The authorities asked Polycarp, "For what harm is there in saying Lord Caesar, and to sacrifice, and thus save your life?" Polycarp was quiet for a long while, then replied, "I will not do it."

They abused him dreadfully and then pushed the godly old man into the stadium. The proconsul saw he was a sickly old man and urged him, "Save your life. Have regard for your age and swear by the genius [the spirit or god] of Caesar." Polycarp refused, saying, "Revile Christ? Eighty and six years have I served Him, and He has never done me wrong, and how can I now blaspheme my King who has saved me?" He was first threatened with being torn apart and devoured by wild beasts. Then he was sentenced to be burned at the stake. Refusing leniency and giving his life for his Lord, that is the death Polycarp faced for not applying the title of lord to Caesar.

Through the centuries, believers by the millions have suffered and bled because they acknowledged Christ as their Savior and Master. And at this very moment, there are myriads more who face torture or even death because they refuse to confess, "Allah is God and Muhammad is his prophet."

In many countries—as documented by the recent books *In the Lion's Den* and *Their Blood Cries Out*—there are multiplied thousands of Christians being jailed, beaten, exiled, and killed because of the "crime" of acknowledging Jesus Christ as Lord and living for Him. For them, there is no dividing line—no separation of Christ's Saviorhood and Lordship. They recognize the biblical teaching that to turn one's life over to Christ means to make Him Master.

THE MEANING OF CHRIST AS LORD

Several years ago, when Bible teacher Charles Stanley was ill in the hospital, he prayed, "Lord, show me something that is practical, something that is brief enough for me to memorize and learn, something to check against my daily life on a practical basis."[7]

During that illness, Stanley wrote down eight principles of Christ's Lordship:

> 1. Jesus Christ is my Lord when I obey the initial promptings of the Holy Spirit without hesitation or argument. In other words, "What He says to you, do it" [see John 2:5].
>
> 2. Jesus Christ is my Lord when I am committed to fulfilling His will for my life before I even know what He will require of me.
>
> 3. Jesus Christ is my Lord when I am available to serve Him without regard to time, space, or circumstances.
>
> 4. Jesus Christ is my Lord when I recognize His ownership of my total life and all of my possessions—and submit to that ownership.
>
> 5. Jesus Christ is my Lord when pleasing Him exceeds my desire to please others.

The psalmist prayed, "I delight to do thy will, O God."

6. Jesus Christ is my Lord when I look to Him as the source of all my needs and desires. God will work out His providential provisions in our lives. He may do that through His divine intervention or He may employ others to fulfill our needs and desires.

7. Jesus Christ is my Lord when I am turning my difficulties and my failures into opportunities for spiritual growth....

8. Jesus Christ is my Lord when to know him intimately becomes the obsession of my life. There must be total commitment, obedience, and availability for His use. Ephesians 6:5 is an admonition to slaves—bondservants, those who were owned by a master.... We do *belong* to the Lord Jesus *if* He is our Lord....[8]

THE HEART OF LORDSHIP: OBEYING GOD

Those who claim to have Jesus as Savior but not necessarily as Lord remind me of the misguided fellow who tried to jolt people with this bizarre statement: "I'm saved, but I'm not a Christian." Frankly, that is just not possible. When a person becomes saved, what is he saved from? His sin. And what is he saved unto? Life in Christ.

While it's true that we as Christians may not always let our lights shine and act in a Christian manner, we are still Christians if we have asked Christ to save us. Believers still make mistakes—that is clear from the struggles Paul described in Romans chapter 7. But the prevalent desire of our hearts is to live as God would have us live and allow Him to conform us "to the image of his Son" (Romans 8:29).

The Clarity of Scripture's Teaching

Ephesians 2:8-9 is perhaps one of the best-known verses proclaiming that salvation is a free gift: "By grace are ye saved through faith; and that not of yourselves: it is the gift of God: not of works, lest any man should boast." But many people overlook the very next verse, which tells us that the result of a saved life is a changed life: "We are his workmanship, created in Christ Jesus *unto good works,* which God hath before ordained that we should walk in them" (verse 10, emphasis added). Obedience does not bring about salvation, but clearly it is the fruit of salvation (see Matthew 3:8, 7:16-20). Moreover, it's evidence of our love for Christ (see John 14:23). Jesus Himself uttered condemnation upon those who worship Him with their lips but not their lives (Matthew 15:7-9).

If it's true that Jesus Christ is our Lord and Savior and has complete, unqualified rulership over our lives, why do we still have a problem with consistently living in total submission to His Lordship? Why do we still succumb to temptation?

Instead of relying on God's infallible Word to answer such questions, people make the serious mistake of using human reason and faulty logic. "Well, since Christians still have a problem with sin, and they are not living perfectly, then it follows that either they have lost their salvation, or...they do not have Jesus as their Lord."

But if Jesus is not your Lord, then neither is He your Savior. Jesus Himself warned:

> Not everyone that saith unto me, Lord, Lord, shall enter into the kingdom of heaven; but he that doeth the will of my father which is in heaven. Many will say to me in that day, Lord, Lord, have we not prophesied in thy name? And in thy name have cast out devils? And in thy name done

many wonderful works? And then profess unto them, I never knew you: depart from me, ye that work iniquity (Matthew 7:21-23).

That passage ought to bring great fear to anyone who professes, "I have Jesus as my Savior but not my Lord."

Fred Wolfe, in his book *The Divine Pattern*, asked, "How can a person obey God?" He answered:

> Obedience does not begin with the outward act. Obedience begins in the heart with the will....There must be a deliberate act of your will if you are going to obey God....There are three choices you have to make with your will if you are going to obey God. First of all, you have to choose to obey God *100 percent*....Second, you must choose to obey God *whether anybody else does or not*....Third, choose to obey Him *no matter what it costs*.[9]

The Cause of People's Confusion

In regard to Christ's Lordship, the Bible seems clear. Why, then, is there such widespread confusion among Christians about this? Let's look at the factors that have contributed to the misunderstandings that prevail today.

1. *To many people, it seems rational and reasonable not to emphasize Lordship salvation because the bulk of Christians live as though Jesus is not their Lord—in fact, not even their Savior.*

Thus, it seems expedient for "lite preachers" to deliver lite messages. These preachers reason, *Most believers live so shabbily it must mean that although they're saved, they just haven't accepted Christ as Lord. So I'm going to preach what I think is logical and appropriate given the way that they are living.*

Who ever said that following God with one's heart, mind, soul, and spirit is logical? To the world, the very rudiments of the gospel are insane, illogical, and impractical (see 1 Corinthians 1:27).

2. *Many Christians feel that the best way to win more people to Christ is to make the gospel appealing to them.*

In this case, a pastor may reason, *If I make this business of discipleship too hard, too demanding, it'll drive people away. People want to go to a church that makes them feel good. So I'd better go light on repentance, sin, judgment, and hell. I believe in what the Bible says about them, but I don't need to talk about them, right? I want to attract people to Christ, not repel them.*

That, however, does not square with the way Jesus Himself led people to salvation. He preached the need for repentance, He declared that to follow Him was to sacrifice everything, and He warned time and again about judgment and hell.

3. *Finally, there are those who flat-out reject the idea that Jesus is both Savior and Lord from the moment of salvation.*

Sadly, those who do not acknowledge Christ's Lordship over their lives bring into question whether they really have come to salvation. It is these people who we're most likely to hear saying, "The demands of Christ in the New Testament are too harsh and were never intended for us moderns. His teachings are good to a point, but through the years certain believers have embellished those accounts. Surely this Jesus, no matter how good a man and teacher He was, could not impose these commands on contemporary Christians. Losing your life? Forsaking all to be His disciple? Taking up one's cross to follow Him? Dying to self? Crucified with Christ? Impossible. Unworkable. Not even requested."

Given those three reasons, it's no wonder the gospel of Christ is not influencing our society today. Ultimately, it's the Lordship of Christ—preached and taught in all of its challenging power—that will draw people to Christ. A watered-down gospel message will not result in a generation of Christians who will steadfastly follow their Lord and Savior to the end. Only those who name Christ as Lord will survive when it comes time for the Judge to separate the wheat from the tares and the good fish from the bad.

ACKNOWLEDGING CHRIST'S LORDSHIP

Jesus Christ is Lord! He is the King of kings and Lord of lords. If you are a bona fide Christian, He is already your Lord. If you have doubts, yield your all to His Lordship and Saviorhood.

> Crown Him with many crowns, the
> Lamb upon His throne;
> Hark! How the heavenly anthem drowns
> all music but its own!
> Awake, my soul, and sing of Him who
> died for Thee,
> And hail Him as Thy matchless King
> through all eternity.
>
> Crown Him the Lord of love! Behold,
> His hands and side—
> Rich wounds, yet visible above, in
> beauty glorified;
> No angel in the sky can fully bear that
> sight,
> But downward bends his wondering eye
> at mysteries so bright.
>
> Crown Him the Lord of life! Who tri-
> umphed o'er the grave;
> Who rose victorious in the strife for
> those He came to save;

His glories now we sing, who died and
    rose on high;
Who died eternal life to bring, and lives
    that death may die.
Crown Him the Lord of heaven! One
    with the Father known,
One with the Spirit through Him given
    yonder glorious throne!
To Thee be endless praise, for Thou for
    us hast died;
But Thou, O Lord, through endless days
    adored and magnified.

—Matthew Bridges

— 3 —

A Hell
Without Reality

It doesn't matter what they preach,
Of high or low degree;
The old hell of the Bible
Is hell enough for me.[1]

—Frank Stanton

Hell.

What response does that word draw from you? Because of the content and intent of this book, most likely you are either a Christian or considering the Christian faith. If you are out and about, you have probably heard that word spoken somewhere during the last week. Or, you may have heard it spoken on the radio or TV set, along with other similar epithets.

Strangely enough, there was a time when the word *hell* was taboo except when enunciated from a pulpit or in a Bible class at a Christian college or a theological seminary.

One recent report by George Barna[2] states that three out of five adults do not believe that Satan exists, not to speak of his dismal domain, hell. According to the Bible, hell is the final place of the unsaved where there is outer darkness (see Matthew 22:13), yet at the same time, fire (see Mark 9:43; Luke 16:24), and weeping and wailing and gnashing of teeth (see Matthew 13:42).

Contemporary society has virtually reduced hell to nothing but a quasi-dirty word. At the same time, the word *hell* is seldom heard from the pulpits of our land. Even large numbers of ministers who believe that hell and the devil exist refrain from preaching on them because their congregations feel uncomfortable about such subjects.

One of my preacher friends conducted the morning service at a county-seat town church. During his sermon entitled "Christ Is the Answer," he merely mentioned that "Jesus entered this world to rescue us from hell and to grant us heaven." After the benediction he was greeting the worshipers at the door. One longtime attendee snorted, "The very idea. We've really heard that 'hellfire-and-damnation' stuff today!"

HELL IS NO JOKE

Hell is one of the most bandied-about words in the English language. Tragically, to most modern Americans hell is nothing but a cuss word and an object of laughter and ridicule. Frequently we see syndicated newspaper cartoons that make light of hell as a joke, picturing masses of people surrounded by flames. How could a conscientious soul discover humor in even the slightest mention of hell? On one side of the spectrum are those who poke fun at the devil and hell—jesting, cartooning, and lampooning these subjects. The fact is that many people want to disarm the appalling truth of hell by laughing at it and fictionalizing it. *Maybe all of this about hell and the devil will go away*, they may think to themselves.

General Sherman's cry of frustration, "War is hell," has echoed for over 130 years. People often refer to their difficult situations as hell. But no matter how dreadful a situation is, it's not hell, nor is it even close. Imagine all of this blighted world's abysmal horrors—the mass destruction of genocide and war, including the persecution and extermination of Jews in the Holocaust and the relentless imprisonment, torture, and execution of Christians in numerous Third World countries; the threatening terrors of nuclear and biological warfare; pestilences like AIDS and other rampaging sexually transmitted diseases; viruses like eboli, ecoli, and their ilk that cause massive hemorrhaging and the rotting of human tissue; cataclysmic upheavals such as earthquakes, hurricanes, tornadoes, floods, and fires—and they pale into insignificance alongside the unspeakably horrible place called hell. There is nothing funny about hell.

> The terrifying consequences of sin include hell, of which Jesus said, "If your right eye makes you stumble, tear it out, and throw it from you; for it is better for you that one of the parts of your body perish, than for your whole body to be thrown into hell" (Matthew 5:30). Scripture describes hell as a dreadful, hideous place where sinners are "tormented with fire and brimstone....And the smoke of their torment goes up forever and ever; and they have no rest day and night" (Revelation 14:10-11). Those truths become all the more alarming when we realize that they are part of the inspired Word of an infinitely merciful and righteous God.[3]

DISTANCING FROM
THE DOCTRINE OF HELL

When is the last time you heard a lesson or sermon on hell? Probably long ago, if at all. In this era of the "consumer-driven" church, a good number of leaders and ministers have gradually backed away from taking the Bible at face value on certain subjects, including condemnation, hell, judgment, homosexuality, and adu'

Most preachers will affirm their belief in the existence of hell, yet they keenly recognize that it is an unpopular subject. The truth hurts. It's far easier to preach on the grace, mercy, and love of God than it is to deal with the devil, hell, and their related ramifications.

Based on the evidence around us, it appears as if the majority of evangelicals have distanced themselves from the doctrine of hell. What sort of effect is this having? Going hand in hand with a disinclination toward hell is the devastating concept of universalism. In other words, if there is no hell—or not much of a hell—perhaps it means that everybody is going to make it into heaven.

> Universalism is the doctrine or the belief that God, through His grace revealed in Christ, will ultimately save every member of the human race from sin, eternal punishment, damnation, and hell regardless of how unrighteous they might have been here on earth....Dr. Roy Fish, professor of evangelism at Southwestern Baptist Theological Seminary, tells of a meeting he attended where four well-known evangelicals were presenting papers on the destiny of the lost. Dr. Fish said that in their presentations, "The word hell was not used one time in that conference. [There was] not one mention of final judgment which consigned unrepentant men to eternal darkness."[4]

WIDESPREAD CONFUSION ABOUT HELL

No Satan, No Hell

Usually, those who do not believe there is a devil or Satan correspondingly do not subscribe to a belief in hell. Satan does not mind this; he is no dummy but rather a clever deceiver (see Revelation 12:9) and the manipulative, murderous father of lies (see John 8:44). He quite frankly would prefer that people renounce the idea of his existence and hell, making those realities seem ludicrous. Even though his power is restricted by God Himself, Lucifer (another one of his names; see Isaiah 14:12) recognizes that the most effective means of luring people into eternal hell is to make them not take seriously the issues of sin, God's judgment, and the prospect of everlasting punishment.

Extreme Views of Hell

There are two additional extremes. There are some people who come to believe in the devil and hell to the extent that they often become involved in Satan and demon worship. Then there are Christians who are so preoccupied with Satan and spiritual warfare that they become emotionally and spiritually paralyzed to the point where they hardly move without thinking about demonic influence and possession. They become trapped by the devil through an obsession with him, feeling he is working in practically everything and everybody. They think the devil and his fallen angels are behind every tree and under every rock, always lurking around every corner.

Sometimes Satan may indeed be lurking around every corner, but he is *not* omnipotent, omnipresent, and omniscient like God. His perverted lust to be all of those—and even to usurp God's power and authority—precipitated God's evicting him and his rebellious angels from heaven (see Isaiah 14:12-15; 2 Peter 2:4). As he roams throughout the earth "as a roaring lion...seeking whom he may devour" (1 Peter 5:8), he is constantly mindful that his ultimate defeat and debasement are imminent.

SATAN IS ALIVE, BUT NOT WELL

Some years ago author Hal Lindsey wrote a book titled *Satan Is Alive and Well on Planet Earth*. While that may be the case, we know that the "old dragon" eventually will lose the war. He was struck a death blow at the cross and at the empty tomb. He is done for—doomed! He is manifestly alive but definitely not well, for he knows his coming fate. At the close of the great tribulation period (and prior to the millennial reign of the Lord Jesus), Satan's cohorts, the beast and the false prophet, will meet this end:

> The best was seized, and with him the false prophet who performed the signs in his presence, by which he deceived those who had received the mark of the beast and those who worshiped his image; these two were thrown alive into the lake of fire which burns with brimstone (Revelation 19:20 NASB).

Then, directly prior to the millennium, Satan will face a precursor of his ultimate banishment and disgrace:

> I saw an angel coming down from heaven, having the key of the abyss and a great chain in his hand. And he laid hold of the dragon, the serpent of old, who is the devil and Satan, and bound him for a thousand years, and threw him into the abyss, and shut it and sealed it over him, so that he should not deceive the nations any longer, until the thousand years were completed; after these things he must be released for a short time (Revelation 20:1-3 NASB).

After Christ's millennial reign on earth the devil will have his last gasp, as he will be released from the pit to command his evil forces against the Lord's army. He and those who follow him will suffer a crushing defeat in which God will send fire from heaven to obliterate them (see

Revelation 20:7-9). Then what will happen to this once-prancing, strutting archenemy of Almighty God and all mankind?

> The devil who deceived them was thrown into the lake of fire and brimstone, where the beast and false prophet are also; and they will be tormented day and night forever and ever (Revelation 20:10 NASB).

And what about those who refused to receive Christ as their Savior and Lord? They will be judged at the Great White Throne, where they will stand before none other than Jesus Christ, the Judge:

> The sea gave up the dead which were in it, and death and Hades gave up the dead which were in them; and they were judged, every one of them according to their deeds. And death and Hades were thrown into the lake of fire. This is the second death, the lake of fire. And if anyone's name was not found written in the book of life, he was thrown into the lake of fire (Revelation 20:13-15 NASB).

Out of loving concern for the lost, then, we must preach both the love and justice of God through Jesus Christ with intensity and power.

WHY CHRIST CAME

Our Lord and Savior is compassionate and loving. He willingly departed the glories of heaven and "pitched His tent among us" (paraphrase of "dwelt" in John 1:14 KJV). From before the foundation of the world it was planned that He was to "save His people from their sins" (Matthew 1:14). That includes saving them from the consequences of those sins—spiritual death and being separated from God in hell for all eternity. As Billy Graham has often explained it, "Jesus Christ went to hell for us."

> The Lord appeared to him from afar, saying, I have loved you with an everlasting love; therefore I have drawn you with lovingkindness (Jeremiah 31:3 NASB).

> God so loved the world, that He gave His only begotten Son, that whoever believes in Him should not perish, but have eternal life (John 3:16 NASB).

> God demonstrates His own love toward us, in that while we were yet sinners, Christ died for us (Romans 5:8 NASB).

> In this is love, not that we loved God, but that He loved us and sent His Son to be the propitiation for our sins....We love, because He first loved us (1 John 4:10,19 NASB).

It is heartbreaking that even in the face of these powerful words about God's love many people still spurn Him—by the millions. How can they reject such love? That is a mystery to every conscientious preacher and teacher of the gospel.

Charles Haddon Spurgeon offered this example of a person who was totally unmoved by fervent preaching:

> A nobleman, skilled in music, who had often observed the Hon. and Rev. Mr. Cadogan's inattention to his performance, said to

him one day, "Come, I am determined to make you feel the force of music; pay particular attention to this piece."

It was accordingly played. "Well, what do you say now?"

"Why, just what I said before."

"What! Can you hear this and not be charmed? Well, I am quite surprised at your insensibility. Where are your ears?"

"Bear with me, my lord," replied Mr. Cadogan, "since I, too, have had my surprise. I have often, from the pulpit, set before you the most striking and affecting truths; I have sounded notes that might have raised the dead; I have said, 'Surely he will feel now,' but you never seem to be charmed with my music, though infinitely more interesting than yours. I, too, have been ready to say, with astonishment, 'Where are your ears?'"[5]

A Crucial Balance

The concerned proponent of God's Word must, to use a dated term, "let it all hang out." That means running the gamut of God's Word, tempering love and mercy with hell and judgment. I have heard this accolade about a number of Christians: "Oh, so-and-so just doesn't [or didn't] have an enemy in the world." Is that really the highest compliment? If a believer is laying it on the line, "speaking the truth in love" (see Ephesians 4:15), he should not expect to be liked by everyone. However, that same believer who lovingly delivers all of God's truth will rank high with God and those who love Him and His Word. And the unsaved who become saved because of his candid words will dearly love him for warning them to "flee from the wrath to come" (see Matthew 3:7) and pointing them to Jesus.

Jude exhorted, "Save others, snatching them out of the fire; and on some have mercy with fear, hating even the garment polluted by the flesh" (verse 23 NASB). The King James Version renders the passage, "And others save with fear, pulling them out of the fire."

So, even more than ever we must preach the entire gospel message—not only "Amazing Grace," but also the gist of the hymn, "Brethren, We Have Met to Worship" by George Atkins:

> Brethren, see poor sinners 'round you
> Slumb'ring on the brink of woe;
> Death is coming, hell is moving,
> Can you bear to let them go?
> See our fathers and our mothers,
> And our children sinking down;
> Brethren, pray, and holy manna
> Will be showered all around.

A CORRECT UNDERSTANDING

Ours Is a Simple Message

In today's complicated society, which is basically confused by sin and its disastrous results, we often hear the opponents of evangelicalism claim that evangelical Christians are "seeking simple answers to complex questions." Exactly! They have read us right. The world sees the gospel as too simple and wants to muddle matters by trying to attach the ungodly trappings of intellectual knowledge, good works, and self-esteem. But only the Savior alone can save.

The plain, unadorned answer to problems still remains the same: Jesus Christ is the only hope for sin-cursed mankind, the only Savior and Deliverer. He is the living Word of God, the *Logos* (see John 1:1-3). He is the absolute embodiment of all truth.

Ours Is a Forthright Message

All around us are those who claim to adhere to Jesus, yet they contradict His very words as recorded in the Scriptures. Many have patently sidestepped the doctrine of hell either because they do not believe hell exists or because they have cold feet about proclaiming the whole counsel of God.

Now notice the rather skewed reasoning of those who claim that all Scripture is to be judged in the light of Jesus Christ and yet, at the same time, either overlook, water down, or deny the fundamental principles found in the Bible. Let me inquire: How do we find out about Jesus Christ? Through the written Word, of course. How do we know that God is a God of love? The Bible. How do we know about His birth, His life, His signs and wonders, His ethical and moral teachings, His views about the kingdom of God, His death, His resurrection, His ascension, His second coming, and heaven and hell? The Bible, most assuredly. Yes, the Holy Spirit can also reveal such things to us, but He cannot and never will operate in contradiction with the parameters of God's written Word.

If we use Scripture to affirm God's love, then we also need to acknowledge what Scripture says about sin, judgment, and hell. Our Lord taught more about hell and judgment than He did about heaven:

> Do not fear those who kill the body, but who are unable to kill the soul; but rather fear Him who is able to destroy both soul and body in hell (Matthew 10:28 NASB).

> The Son of Man...will cast them into the furnace of fire; in that place there shall be weeping and gnashing of teeth (Matthew 13:41-42 NASB).

> It is better for you to lose one part of
> your body than for your whole body to be
> thrown into hell (Matthew 5:29, NIV).

How would many of today's public-relations conscious congregations respond to a preacher who related a blood-curdling "deathbed story" about a person who actually went to hell? And suppose that preacher went into detail about the torment, the remorse, the flames, the anguish, the thirst, and the loneliness of that place. He would probably be asked not to speak of such things lest newcomers be frightened away. And longtime attendees might even express their disdain by holding back on their service or giving.

But our loving, merciful Lord taught exactly such a story in Luke chapter 16, where He related the account concerning a rich man and a poor beggar, Lazarus. Look at the specifics of what He said:

> In Hades [hell prior to the resurrection
> of the unsaved dead] he [the rich man] lifted
> up his eyes, being in torment, and saw
> Abraham far away, and Lazarus in his bosom
> [to the Jewish mind, Abraham's bosom
> represented heaven, the place of the saved
> dead].
>
> And he cried out and said, "Father
> Abraham, have mercy on me, and send
> Lazarus, that he may dip the tip of his finger
> in water and cool off my tongue; for I am in
> agony in this flame" (verses 23-24 NASB).

Father Abraham, in kindness, called the rich man "child" (verse 25), and reminded him that in the previous life he had been the recipient of good, whereas Lazarus had had a rough life. But now the tables had been turned: Lazarus was comfortable, and the rich man was in agony and torment. Then Abraham explained that there was a tremendous chasm between his bosom and Hades—a chasm so great that no one could cross over it (see verses 25-26).

The rich man then asked Abraham about his brothers back on earth:

> He said, "Then I beg you, Father, that you send him [Lazarus] to my father's house—for I have five brothers—that he may warn them, lest they also come to this place of torment."
>
> But Abraham said, "They have Moses and the Prophets; let them hear them."
>
> But he said, "No, Father Abraham, but if someone goes to them from the dead, they will repent!"
>
> But he said to him, "If they do not listen to Moses and the Prophets, neither will they be persuaded if someone rises from the dead" (verses 27-31 NASB).

Like untold numbers of people throughout history, the rich man wanted a special dispensation. "Send Lazarus over to give me a drop of water." When that failed, he turned to a request for his unsaved brothers: "Raise Lazarus and send him to my five brothers so that he can warn them up here." Yet Abraham revealed how hard-hearted people can be. He pointed out that obstinate unbelievers would not believe even if someone rose from the dead and preached to them. After all, Jesus Himself rose from the dead and multitudes still turned Him down with cold callousness.

Regardless of what is done, the majority of mankind will not respond to the grace, love, mercy, and tenderness of God. On one occasion our Lord answered His Jewish critics by stating:

> You search the Scriptures, because you
> think that in them you have eternal life; *and
> it is these that bear witness of Me....*Do not
> think that I will accuse you before the
> Father; the one who accuses you is Moses,
> in whom you have set your hope. For if you
> believed Moses, you would believe Me; for
> *he wrote of Me. But if you do not believe his
> writings, how will you believe My words?*
> (John 5:39, 45-47 NASB, emphasis added).

If a person has true saving faith in Jesus, doesn't it follow that he will believe Jesus' words in the Scriptures? That definitely includes not only Jesus' words pertaining to God as Lover of the entire world, but also His words about God as Judge.

If you're a follower of the Lord Jesus Christ, you want to please Him. You want to walk in His steps. You want to glorify, magnify, and praise Him—right? Then the optimum course of action for you is to proclaim His truth—no matter how much it hurts, no matter how unpleasant it may seem.

COMPASSION DEMANDS
PREACHING ON HELL

We should never preach or teach about hell unless there is a pain in our heart and a sob in our throat. Concern for the lost should make us agonize and weep. Paul cried, "Brethren, my heart's desire and prayer to God for Israel is, that they might be saved" (Romans 10:1).

Paul also testified that he wished he could go to hell in place of the Jews, his brothers and sisters in the flesh, so that they could know salvation. Of course we know that wouldn't have been possible, but his statement reveals to us the great burden on his heart:

> I say the truth in Christ, I lie not, my
> conscience also bearing me witness in the
> Holy Ghost, that I have great heaviness and
> continual sorrow in my heart. For I could
> wish that myself were accursed from Christ
> for my brethren, my kinsmen according to
> the flesh (Romans 9:1-3).

Moses expressed similarly intense emotions after he returned from receiving the Ten Commandments on Mount Sinai. He was wounded to the soul when his eyes beheld the drunken, naked people of Israel dancing around a golden calf fashioned after the Egyptian bull-god Apis. He poured out his spirit before the Lord God:

> Now, if Thou wilt, forgive their sin—
> and if not, please blot me out from Thy
> book which Thou hast written! (Exodus
> 32:32 NASB).

Moses was no doubt referring to the book of life. Can you imagine such passion. Would you be willing to forfeit heaven and spend eternity enduring the indescribable horrors of hell for anyone, even your closest relatives? Thank God, you and I can't and won't have to, for Christ has already paid the price to redeem you and me, freeing us from the shackles of Satan and translating us from the devil's kingdom "into the kingdom of his dear Son" (Colossians 1:13).

Jeremiah was called "the weeping prophet," and not without reason. He not only proclaimed the truth to the wayward people of God, but he wept profusely over their backslidden condition. He lamented:

> Oh, that my head were waters,
> And my eyes a fountain of tears,

That I might weep day and night
For the slain of the daughter of my people!
(Jeremiah 9:1 NASB).

Many evangelical Christians today are not of the same sentiment. They are not actively involved in rescuing people from hell either because they are too busy with their own concerns, they feel awkward about sharing the gospel, or they consider themselves too "sophisticated" to deal with hell and the devil.

Dr. W. A. Criswell asked the question, "What is it that produces compassion?" One of his answers was this:

> *The nature of hell.* I still believe in a darkened, lonely, tragic place called hell. I do not purport to understand it. But the Book teaches it, and I know that somehow, in the divine economy, men who refuse Christ here will spend eternity shamefully and horribly separated from God and from every flaunted expression of His grace. Not even my most verbose antagonist do I wish to see in hell. Knowing about hell should make us love men.[6]

I repeat: many Christians have argued that you can't reach people by preaching on hell. They say we should just touch them through love. But genuine, heaven-generated love calls for us to tell the truth—to tell it like it is. We are sinning against a lost world if we do not inform people where they are going if they reject Jesus Christ as Savior.

British poet James Russell Lowell, a Christian, penned these heart-gripping lines about a person in hell:

I plead today from hell's cruel fire
And tell you now my last desire.

You cannot do a thing for me...
　　No words today, my bonds will free.

But do not err, my friend again;
　　Do all you can for the souls of men.

Plead with them now quite earnestly,
　　Lest they be cast in hell with me.

Christian, if the eternal hopelessness of all those who go to hell does not motivate you to win souls, nothing else will. It is this very hopelessness your loved ones, friends, neighbors, and work associates will suffer if they do not receive Christ into their life. How can we profess to be concerned and, at the same time, remain silent about Satan and hell?

We are accountable to God for our absence of genuine concern and compassion!

— 4 —

A People
Without Purity

*What can the church do? First, we need to make
a credible case that Christianity can fill [people's]
hunger. We must develop a cultural apologetic
showing the positive social benefits of Christianity. We don't have to bang anyone on the
head with a Bible; we can simply present the
facts. Statistics show that Christian marriages
are stronger, that kids raised in the church are
more likely to resist sex and drugs, that crime
recedes when spiritual values are ascendant.*

*Second, we need to argue that Christianity is not
just good for society, it is the truth. Contrary to
some church-growth experts, the secret is not to
attract people by making them feel good. The ther-
apeutic appeal is as bankrupt in the church as it is
in the culture at large.... then we must give them
what only the church can give: a message of truth
and meaning, based on the One who is Truth.*

—Charles Colson[1]

Does it appear strange that those who are outside of
Christ and His church have few qualms about engaging in
sinful behavior yet at the same time are quick to denounce

Christians who are found to commit the same sinful actions? The popular perception of society is that it's okay to cheat a little on a tax form, but if a minister or Christian organization errs in its financial accountability—even unintentionally—there's typically an outcry. Most people don't give a second thought about telling a lie, but if a Christian is caught telling a lie, it's a blight against his reputation. His lie is remembered for a long time afterward, while the lie from an unbeliever oftentimes goes unchallenged and is quickly forgotten.

Does this double standard seem unfair? Some may think so, but frankly, the world has every reason to hold Christians to a higher standard. In fact, we should *want* for society to recognize that the followers of Jesus Christ hold to a vastly different set of values. Yes, it's true that the world often goes to the extreme and expects Christians to be perfect, and we know that's unrealistic. But the general pattern of our lives should be such that it's clear there's something different about us. The apostle Paul, in Philippians 2:15, commanded that we "be blameless and harmless, the sons of God, without rebuke, in the midst of a crooked and perverse nation, among whom ye shine as lights in the world." In the darkness of night, a shining light cannot be missed. What about us as Christians? Does the world notice us in contrast to the surrounding darkness?

PURITY OF PROCLAMATION

When I speak of purity, I am concerned not only about our obligation to live pure lives as believers, but also the purity of the gospel message that we proclaim. Are we presenting the whole counsel of God's Word? Or are we concerned that certain Bible teachings or passages will turn people off?

Purity in proclamation means telling people about both sides of the gospel coin. Today, unbelievers are invited to find peace, joy, and fulfillment in Christ, but little or nothing is said about why it is necessary to come to Christ—that people need to be saved from their sins. More and more, Christians are becoming hesitant to tell an unsaved person that he or she is spiritually "dead in trespasses and sins" (Ephesians 2:1). Yet that's the only way people are going to realize their need for Christ. Repentance is a necessary part of conversion—the person receiving Christ needs to declare his intention to *turn away* from sin and *follow* Jesus.

John A. Mackay, a staunch Presbyterian educator of a bygone era, said it well:

> The Gospel of God is to be proclaimed in the background of bad news. The Gospel is Good News about God, but in the background there is very bad news about man. And I venture to say that the Good News about God will never be appreciated unless the bad news about man is understood and taken into account. The news about man is bad, and at the present moment it simply couldn't be worse....
>
> Another part of the good-bad news is that this rift has, in our time, produced a literally appalling void....This utter emptiness, lack of light, lack of meaning, anonymity, banality, loneliness, in low places and high places, around the globe today—this eerie emptiness, creating a problem for light and for life to illumine the abyss.... How is the Gospel, then, to be proclaimed? It is to be proclaimed in the background of bad news; it is to be proclaimed to all men everywhere.[2]

A FAITHFUL PERSISTENCE

There are also those who say that the world is so far gone that we can't reach people for Christ anymore. They say that Jesus warned that the world would get worse and worse toward the end, and that we may as well not bother with proclaiming the gospel because people are going to reject it anyway.

But didn't Jesus say, "Occupy till I come"? (Luke 19:13). We are called to keep presenting the pure, unadulterated Word of God until the moment that the Lord Himself comes to rapture His bride, the church. Christ is still in the business of saving people. Just because society seems to be descending rapidly in an irreversible downward spiral doesn't mean we should give up. While it's true that conditions are worsening all around us, we need to remember that millions of people worldwide have placed Christ on the throne of their hearts. And there are many more whom God will draw to Himself—many who, even at this moment, are on the verge of making a decision. We do not want to be negligent with the opportunities God has given us in the here and now.

A DOWNFALL BEGINS WITH COMPROMISE

What's to blame for the poor state of society today? It's not necessarily as complex as we might think; while there are several factors, there's one that's particularly ironic: all too many pastors, teachers, missionaries, and church members are proclaiming the *lite gospel*. Their proclamation is often tainted and impure.

There's no doubt we can trace one phase of our nation's decline to Madalyn Murray O'Hair's atheistic insistence that led to the Supreme Court's ruling to ban prayer and Bible reading from public schools. Another significant contributing factor is the same court's decision in Roe vs. Wade, which legalized abortion per our court system—a decision that runs contrary to the Court that really matters—God's judgment hall.

We can also blame part of the problem on a public education system that, in accord with the desires of the

National Education Association (NEA), has basically espoused the removal of all Judeo-Christian moral values from school curricula, the elimination of creationism as a viable view of the universe's origin, and the propagation of "diversity" teachings that go beyond the acceptance of people of other races and cultures (which we as Christians should practice) and promote alternative sexual lifestyles (which are clearly prohibited in the Bible).

There are a number of other major reasons for the massive decline taking place in our country today. But we cannot place all the blame elsewhere. I believe the church has actually helped to perpetuate this decline rather than slow it.

Emile Zola, a novelist in nineteenth-century France, wrote a famous book entitled *J'accuse*, which means, "I accuse." I accuse us Christians—and I accept part of the blame—as among the main offenders in society's ethical and moral avalanche downward. The prophetic books of the Old Testament (such as Isaiah, Jeremiah, and Ezekiel) describe the nation of Israel shortly before God poured out His wrath upon the people. What's stunning is that the very same sins that brought God's judgment upon Israel are rampant today in America.

Now, the hardhearted apathy of the Israelites didn't develop overnight; it grew gradually. It started with one compromise, then another, then another. And the church today is on that same slippery slope. We've made a small compromise here, and another one there—especially in the area of how we handle the Bible. We've gone from being a church that clings firmly to the whole counsel of God's Word and we've become selective in our approach to presenting and interpreting Scripture. This has left the church with a lite gospel that lacks the power to convict people of their sins and truly change their lives.

This gradual slipping away from God's Word manifests itself in a number of ways. Some Christians make devotional or inspirational books their main diet, neglecting the discipline of feasting upon and memorizing Scripture so that it may permeate their lives. In other words, their spiritual nourishment is secondhand rather than firsthand. There's nothing wrong with reading good Christian books, but above all else, our time in God's Word needs to come first. After all, it's the Bible that equips us with everything we need for the Christian life (see 2 Timothy 3:16).

In addition, there are many pastors who read just one verse or even part of a verse in their messages and never refer to the Scriptures again. You'll see this on Christian television, where many of the speakers proclaim content that is loosely based on the Bible yet don't back up their statements with specific scripture references. Consider the people who sit under such teachers—what view do you think they'll have of God's Word? Will they see Scripture as the plumb line against which everything in life should be measured?

What happens to Christians who aren't firmly rooted in the Word? We may see an initial burst of enthusiasm in their lives, but it will be a zeal that's not according to knowledge. They won't have, in their minds and hearts, the scriptural information that will sustain them through life's hard moments and challenges. They won't be ready with an answer for those who ask hard questions about life. Most important of all, the shallowness of their interaction with God's Word will become clearly evident in their words and actions. Unsaved people won't see these Christians as very distinct from the world—and thus will assume that there's not much of a difference between a believer and an unbeliever. In fact, there are Christians who are embarrassed to admit to their faith—they take the light God has given them and "put it under a bushel" (Matthew 5:15).

THE DAMAGE CAUSED BY INCONSISTENCY

The most damaging blow of all to the cause of Christ is Christians who adhere to God's Word and proclaim it, but manifest attitudes and actions that are inconsistent with the teachings of Scripture. This isn't anything new; the apostle Paul had to deal with this problem in the New Testament church. Many of his rebukes were directed at individuals who professed to follow Christ yet carried a lot of their sinful, pre-salvation baggage into the church.

Some Christians try to justify their inconsistent testimony by saying, "Well, Jesus is the only one who is perfect. Because I can't be morally and ethically flawless in this life, I'll just sort of drift along." Then there are Christians who presume heavily on God's love, grace, and mercy. They conclude that because God loves them and will always forgive them, there's no reason to be overly concerned about indulging in sin every now and then. "God understands," they say. "He knows how hard it is for us to live the Christian life. He doesn't expect us to be perfect."

No, God doesn't expect perfection, but neither does He want us to have a casual attitude about sin in our lives. Scripture is clear on this point:

> It is written, Be ye holy; for I am holy (1 Peter 1:16).

> Consider the members of your earthly body as dead to immorality, impurity, passion, evil desire, and greed....[and] put on the new self who is being renewed to a true knowledge according to the image of the One who created him (Colossians 3:5,10 NASB).

> Let not sin therefore reign in your mortal body, that ye should obey it in the lusts thereof. Neither yield ye your members as instruments of unrighteousness unto sin: but yield yourselves unto God....As ye [formerly] yielded your members servants to

> uncleanness and to iniquity unto iniquity;
> even so now yield your members servants
> to righteousness unto holiness (Romans
> 6:12-13,19).

Given the choice to sin, we are to be holy, to count ourselves as dead to sin, and yield ourselves to righteousness rather than unrighteousness. And while it's true that God loves us and forgives us, we must not forget that sin deeply grieves Him and renders us ineffective for the work He has called us to do. We cannot take sin lightly; and we cannot allow ourselves to fall under the delusion that the world doesn't really care what we do as Christians. The world *is* paying attention, and when unsaved people see believers who take sin lightly, the unsaved people, in turn, come to take sin lightly as well.

THE DANGER CAUSED BY MISCONCEPTIONS

Another way that Christians have done a disfavor to the world is to spread the misconception that the Christian life is a snap—that when you accept Jesus, life will go smoothly and you'll never have any problems again. But that's not the case.

One night when he was launching into his message, Billy Graham asked the crowd, "Now, all of you who are bothered by the devil, please raise your hands." Out of the vast throng, only a few hands were raised. Then Billy said, "Well, those of you who didn't raise your hands must not be Christians, because the moment you turn to Christ, the devil will bother you and fight and oppose you the rest of your life!"

Yes, we are saved and kept by God's grace, and it's impossible for us to lose our salvation, but still we are in a spiritual battle that will continue for as long as we live out the salvation which God works in us (see Philippians 2:12-13). While you are protected by Christ's shed blood and

Satan can never again own you, still he will do everything he can to mess up your life and keep you from drawing other people to Christ. That's why the apostle Paul alerted us concerning the weapons of warfare:

> Put on the whole armor of God, that ye may be able to stand against the wiles of the devil. For we wrestle not against flesh and blood, but against principalities, against powers, against the rulers of the darkness of this world, against spiritual wickedness in high places (Ephesians 6:11-12).

I have read and heard so many times that living a victorious Christian life is elementary. "Christ has won the battle for us," we are told. "All we have to do is claim His victory." While that may be true in terms of our salvation and eternal destiny, the reality is that we're going to find ourselves involved in spiritual warfare just about every day of our lives. It's when we forget these daily battles that we let our guard down and become vulnerable to the temptations and snares of the world. Ephesians 6:11-12 treats the battle as one that's very real; we need to stand strong because there's a lot at stake—a world that's watching close to see if Christianity is for real.

THE NEED TO ENFORCE PURITY

I have often said that one of the easiest organizations in the world to join is a church. That may sound great at first, but let's think this through for a moment. There are many people who are able to become church members merely on their own word. They may say they're already a Christian, they may try to enter a church by transferring their membership from another place, and oftentimes they aren't questioned about the authenticity of their faith. Few churches are willing to ask what needs to be asked: "Are you really born again? Have you really accepted Christ as your Lord and Savior? How do you know you're saved?"

The reason this is a problem is because many people are becoming members when they're not really saved in the first place. Over time, a church's membership can end up being comprised of people who are ignorant about the saving gospel message of Jesus Christ and what it really means to be a Christian. This, in turn, weakens the church's witness to the world.

Consider, by contrast, other organizations, such as civic clubs like the Lions, the Rotary Club, the Kiwanis, and so on. If a member stops attending the club functions, eventually the club contacts the member and inquires about his absence. They ask, "Do you want to continue as a member?" What's more, every member in such clubs is expected to pay annual or monthly dues—it's an obligation, not an option. Imagine the furor that would arise if churches were to begin charging mandatory dues!

In many churches, then, it's possible to be absent, give nothing, and do nothing, and yet remain on the membership roll! If a Christian displays such a total lack of commitment to the church—which is the body of Christ—then you can be sure there's also a lack of commitment in the way he or she lives the Christian life before a watching world.

Another way we do disservice to God's church is by neglecting to deal with Christians who, for one reason or another, are actively indulging in a lifestyle of sin. There are three possible explanations for what is happening in the life of such a person: 1) he lives in sin because he never became saved in the first place; 2) he lives in sin because he hasn't been instructed to the point that he can recognize his wrongdoing; or 3) he really is saved yet has chosen to live in sin, and no one has made an effort to confront him about his behavior.

While all three situations are different, they all stem from the same problem: Churches today are not following up in the lives of the people who attend regularly. They are not taking the time to ensure that new members truly are saved, and they're not offering classes that help new Christians to "grow in grace, and in the knowledge of our Lord and Savior Jesus Christ" (2 Peter 3:18). And many church leaders are reluctant to say anything to a church member who is living in rebellion. They usually ignore the problem, hoping it will go away on its own. But that's the worst thing they can do. Ignoring sin in the church will give unbelievers a wrong impression of the church, and will communicate to believers that sin must not be a very serious matter.

Why is there a dearth of spiritual purity in churches today? It's because the holy, pure, and righteous standards of God are not being upheld. Rather than emphasize repentance, holiness, purity, and righteousness, many pastors and teachers would rather deal with non-confrontational topics. One reason for this is because they are afraid that they'll turn off unbelievers. Unfortunately, in the attempt to make non-Christians comfortable, they sacrifice the opportunity to bring these same people to Christ. O. S. Hawkins, in his book titled *Where Angels Fear to Tread*, makes this observation:

> When was the last time you turned on your television set to hear a preacher of the gospel thundering forth the message of repentance? When was the last time you read a book on the need of repentance? Pulpits and preachers are strangely silent today regarding the message of repentance.
>
> There are many preachers today who are soothingly, softly whispering "believe, believe, believe." This positive preaching is

> popular because it calls for no change of
> life-style. While many whisper "believe,"
> too few are proclaiming the message of the
> Bible, "Repent." [3]

Ultimately, it's a no-win situation for the church: When we fail to tell unbelievers about their need to turn from sin, we end up de-emphasizing the problem of sin altogether. When we neglect to proclaim sin as a serious affront to God, the church attendees who are true believers can easily end up thinking that sin isn't all that harmful.

It's now to the point that I've heard of men who profess to be Christians trying to excuse their sexually immoral behavior by using David as an example. They argue, "Look at what David did with Bathsheba, and he was a man after God's own heart!" Yes, David had an adulterous relationship, but he *repented* of his actions—and still, untold grief and chastisement fell upon him and his family. A number of Bible scholars point out that David was not the same man after his affair with Bathsheba. The rest of his kingship was full of strife. The baby born to David and Bathsheba died. David's son Absalom tried to usurp David's throne, and ended up being executed by Abner, David's army captain. Various people around David turned on him. And David's long-awaited dream of seeing the Temple built under his reign was not realized. Instead, the Temple was built during the monarchy of one of his sons, Solomon.

We cannot excuse sin simply because great Bible characters such as Abraham, Moses, and David fell at one time or another. Their sinful actions were the exception, not the rule. They made mistakes, but by and large, their lives were lived in wholehearted obedience to God's commands. Though they failed at times, they lived in constant pursuit of godliness. By contrast, there are many today who profess to be Christians but live in such a way that they don't stand out in the midst of the unbelievers around them.

As we noted earlier, no Christian is perfect. Every truly repentant person will, from time to time, be enticed by the devil to return to his former sins. That's what happened to the Israelites after they fled Egypt—when they got tired of eating manna in the wilderness, they complained to Moses and wished they could go back to Egypt because they missed "the cucumbers, and the melons, and the leeks, and the onions, and the garlic" (Numbers 11:5). And remember when the Israelites asked Aaron to fashion the golden calf? Although they had been oppressed as slaves in Egypt, apparently they had enjoyed the orgies that had accompanied the worship of Isis, Apis (the bull god), and other false deities. Though the Israelites were now free from bondage, they missed certain elements of their past.

Many times, Christians who have struggled with a particular weakness in their life have told me that the pull to sin is so strong they can hardly stand it. I try to encourage them by reminding them of God's incredible promise in 1 Corinthians 10:13:

> There hath no temptation taken you but such as is common to man: but God is faithful, who will not suffer you to be tempted above that ye are able; but will with the temptation also make a way to escape, that ye may be able to bear it.

WHAT IS THE SOLUTION?

Years ago, it was fairly common for pastors (and their lay people) to preach harshly about things that people shouldn't do. You would hear sermons about clothing, jewelry, makeup, substance abuse, sexual immorality, and so on. Many churches promoted a gospel of "Don't do this, don't do this, don't do that." The focus was on everything that a person could do wrong—which, of course, made unbelievers uncomfortable. The soul harvest in these kinds of churches was minimal because they were trying to change people's outer behavior rather than their hearts.

So I can understand the people today who say we need to be sensitive to unbelievers and be careful lest we turn them off. However, I believe we've gone too far to the opposite extreme: We've tried to accommodate sinners to the point that we no longer want to confront them about what's wrong in their lives. In our desire to make unbelievers feel welcome, we've de-emphasized the problem of sin, which inevitably leaves us in the position of de-emphasizing the call for people to live righteous, holy lives.

So what's the solution? We certainly don't want unbelievers to view the church as uncaring, unloving, and unfeeling. We want them to be attracted to God. Yet at the same time, if we really love and care for unbelievers, we will do whatever is necessary to save them from a life of disgrace, shame, pain, and destruction. We will do whatever it takes to keep them out of hell—and that means sharing the gospel in its fullness. That means letting them know what the Bible says about sin. Only then will they have the information they need in order to become truly converted.

I'm not sure why, but when the subject of purity comes up, some Christians get the impression it has to do with being stern, humorless, and holier-than-thou. But that's not the case at all! Some of the zaniest, most fun-filled people in the world are Christians. We who are believers have every valid reason to be that way—every season 'tis the season to be jolly because we are possessed with "joy unspeakable and full of glory" (1 Peter 1:18). We are secure in Christ and bound for heaven, and we are enjoying a "foretaste of glory divine" right now. We have been saved, are set apart, and with God's help, becoming more and more Christlike as the days pass.

Encouraging Purity in Ourselves and Others

What can you and I do to encourage purity in the lives of those within the church?

1. We ourselves must exemplify lives of purity in thought, speech, attitude, and action. Purity means that we will not adulterate (defile, debase, pollute, or make impure) our personal selves or the lives of others. Living in purity, with a clear conscience, is a glorious thrill. Talk about being free! There is nothing that equals the boundless freedom we experience when we stand clean and pure before the Lord.

When our "sins are confessed up," as the late missionary heroine Bertha Smith put it, we don't have to keep looking over our shoulder and worrying that we will embarrass our Lord and let down the people depending upon and watching us.

2. In a spirit of firm love (some call it "tough love") we should expect high standards not only from our church staff members, including the pastor, but from the entire membership. We cannot be "moral policemen." If we were, we would need many—maybe hundreds—of full-time church cops to keep up with even a fraction of the shenanigans in the lives of those who profess Christ. Yet we can insist on a constitution and by-laws that spell out New Testament qualifications for church leaders and righteous behavior on the part of the membership at large.

3. When we notice disturbing trends in the church, we should raise questions discreetly and judiciously. I would not dare attempt to specify all of the dangerous shiftings possible, but they are numerous. For example, what are the children and youth being taught about the Christian view of love and marriage?

Are people ever suggesting that, in order to maintain or build the current church membership, the church must condone un-Christian behavior, such as men and women who are living together? Is there a tendency to lean too far in the direction of the lost world under the guise of "reaching people"?

4. Are biblical standards consistently being taught in the Bible classes and preached from the pulpit? If your pastor and church leaders are not speaking out for the highest of values—and they are intent on proclaiming a lite gospel—you may need to evaluate your continued involvement in the church.

Standing Firm for God

There's a short story I once heard that illustrates well what happens when we compromise our original intentions:

A man starting in the fish business hung out a sign that read, "Fresh Fish for Sale Today." He invited his friends to come for the grand opening. They all congratulated him on his enterprise, but one person suggested that the sign could be improved. He said, "Why use the word 'Today'? Of course it's today, and not yesterday or tomorrow."

So the fishmonger removed the word. Then another friend said, "Why have the phrase, 'for sale'? Everyone will

know that because this is a store, your stock is for sale."
And off came the words.

Yet another person complained, "Why the word 'fresh'?
Your integrity guarantees every fish to be fresh."

Finally, only the word "Fish" remained, but someone
objected, "Why the sign? I smelled your fish two blocks
away!" [4]

The church that tries to please everyone will end up
pleasing no one. Put up your sign, and stand by it!

— 5 —

A Church
Without Compassion

Jesus' compassion in us will surely lead us to reach out to the special cases of needs around us—the alcoholic, the mentally and emotionally disturbed, the battered and abused child and adult, the handicapped, the single parent, those who have family problems, the homosexual, those with AIDS and the juvenile delinquent, among others. Like the good Samaritan, our compassion will move us to get off our horse, bend down and bind up the wounds of the suffering people all around us.[1]

—E. W. Price, Jr.

Many churches that call themselves "Christian" in their attitudes and actions are far from being devoted followers of the Lord Jesus Christ.

If there is a place where hurting, wounded persons can turn for compassion and love, it should be a church, whether a mission down a dusty road seemingly miles from nowhere or a massive city megachurch where 10,000 or more people gather on a Sunday morning.

When I was in the pastorate, many members and nonmembers confided to me, "Brother Bailey, in this church I have found real love." Others testified similarly, "Preacher, this is the only place where anybody has ever said to me, 'I love you.'"

Oftentimes these people came from abusive family relationships, where they had been kicked out or ostracized by their own families—battered wives; love-starved husbands; teenagers who were literally booted out of their homes, cursed, and commanded never to come back.

We used to sing "Where Could I Go But to the Lord?" Yes, there is no other place to go. Only in Him will we ever find salvation and all the wonders that accompany redemption—the forgiveness of sins; peace of heart, mind, and soul; eternal security, a "foretaste of glory divine"; spiritual blessings beyond expression; and all of the fruit of the Spirit.

REFLECTING CHRIST'S COMPASSION

Who is supposed to represent the Lord? His church—every born-again believer on the face of the earth. If people want to see what God is like, the only way they can do so is by reading the Bible, or watching the lives of Christians. Since most unbelievers have no interest in reading the Bible, we who are Christians are the only opportunity people have to see God, who is on display through the works He does in our lives. That brings us to an important question: How clearly can unbelievers see God through your life? How clearly can they see Him through your church? Are you and your church offering a clear view of God?

All across the countryside are signs like...

First Church
Welcome

Evangelistic Temple
A Place Where Jesus Is Real

Fellowship Community Church
Where God's Word Is Taught

Suppose Mr. Seeking Sinner visits one of the services at First Church and discovers he is really not welcome, contrary to the church sign. It is as though he does not exist, that he is the invisible man. Some people might even stare at him as though to say, "What are you doing in here? You're not one of us."

Maybe a few isolated members in the church know that they should reach out to this seeking sinner, but they decide not to bother, for they do not want to "rock the boat" and upset the other members. Besides, they've heard the argument for not accepting strangers into the fellowship: "Look, those people are not our kind of folks! We don't want to make them feel welcome here; they will do nothing but cause us inconvenience and cost us money. It's better to just ignore them so they'll go away."

By contrast, the Lord Jesus had open arms for all people, regardless of their economic, social, and spiritual conditions. Our loving Savior still calls out:

> Come unto me, all ye that labor and are
> heavy laden, and I will give you rest. Take
> my yoke upon you, and learn of me; for I am
> meek and lowly in heart: and ye shall find
> rest unto your souls. For my yoke is easy,
> and my burden is light (Matthew 11:28-30).

Next, we see Mr. Seeking Sinner visit the Evangelistic Temple, "a place where Jesus is [allegedly] real." There the service's participants vociferously shout out their holiness and piety and showcase their 100-decibel-plus music and elaborate performance choreography. The service is an extravaganza that so focuses on displays of human "talent" and ego that Jesus is definitely not the real focal point of the service.

These worshipers are so caught up in the excitement and euphoria that they don't notice Mr. Seeking Sinner. Then when it comes time for the preacher to deliver the message, he puts on a dramatic performance as well, citing very little of God's Word. As Mr. Seeking Sinner slinks out, he is left with one impression: "They really move around a lot in that church, but I don't think Jesus was very real."

Now let's go to Fellowship Community Church. Mr. Seeking Sinner, in a last-gasp effort, sneaks into the back of the sanctuary (*mortuary* would be a better word). The church is in direct contrast to Evangelistic Temple. The three carefully selected hymns, which are listed on a little board on the front wall, are sung with the gusto of a choking man who desperately needs the Heimlich maneuver. The service moves with all the energy of a bilious turtle or a crippled snail. The minister, who is obsessed with looking prim and proper, is very subdued and periodically clears his throat in a professorial manner. However, we should thank the Lord that he at least quotes from the Bible. But this minister teaches the most exciting book in the universe as though it were a funeral dirge. And worse, Mr. Sinner, the one visitor this morning, is not acknowledged or welcomed. Visitors at Fellowship Community Church aren't easy to miss, for they stick out like the proverbial sore thumb because they are few and far between.

THE LACKING FACTOR

It seems the missing ingredient in all of those churches is compassion—genuine concern, caring, and kindness. All three of those characteristics were very much on display in the Lord Jesus Christ. And isn't the church to reflect the same characteristics?

The late Ramsey Pollard, predecessor to Adrian Rogers at Bellevue Baptist Church, Memphis, wrote:

The curse of modern-day preaching is the shameful lack of compassion. Too many preachers are calm expositors of truth rather than impassioned preachers of the gospel.

We have allowed intellectual pride to stifle heart power. We have allowed ourselves to be laughed out of our enthusiasm. We have let the devil convince us that if compassion and zeal are elements in our preaching, some "highbrow" will point the finger of scorn and contempt in our direction and pronounce that we are emotional, and therefore, lacking in intelligence.

There is no conflict between intelligence and emotion. Paul had both; and, if we are to be worthy witnesses for Christ, we must have something to say, and we must deliver our souls with compassionate zeal....[2]

My prayer is that your church is not similar to the three hypothetical churches I have mentioned. To repeat the title of a book I read, *The Church Is People*.[3] Why are churches the way they are? Why do they assume certain characteristics, good and bad, sublime and sinful? The individual people, of course.

It usually starts with the pastor and the leadership, and filters down to the people. In some instances, new pastors, teachers, or lay people will unwarily enter a situation where the cold, concrete-like character of the church has been molded for so long there is practically nothing that can be done—no matter how hard one tries—to change the un-Christian attitudes that have progressively become worse over the generations. In some of the churches, if a pastor or the staff members were to try to put the sacred cows out to pasture, they would be assuring themselves of immediate dismissal.

A LOSS OF CONCERN

I was appalled to discover recently that, according to the latest statistics, one of the more evangelistic denominations in our country has more than 10,000 churches that reported no baptisms in the last year! In other words, in those 10,000 churches no new lives were brought to Christ and brought forward to be baptized. And that's just in one denomination! I find it difficult to imagine that many worshiping without adding new Christians to the flock.

Nearly all of these baptism-less "lighthouses" have a rationale—actually, an alibi. "We're in a changing community." Or, "We're now in the inner-city" (yet research shows they really may be 10 to 15 miles from the actual inner-city). "We're in a declining area." "We grew spiritually all year, but there were simply no professions of faith—thus, no baptisms." "We have no prospects." I speak in the utmost love when I say this, but many times those explanations are not legitimate.

Is it possible that the majority of those churches are devoid of Christ's compassion? They sing, "Rescue the perishing, care for the dying, snatch them in pity from sin and the grave. Weep o'er the erring ones, lift up the fallen. Tell them of Jesus, the mighty to save." But it appears there's not much rescuing, caring, snatching in pity, weeping, lifting, and telling!

Churches characterized by a lack of compassion run the gamut of rural, village, town, and city churches. But they usually possess one or more of these deadening traits:

> • A pastor and/or staff that is "professional" and lackadaisical and has the mistaken idea that they exist merely to "equip the saints" and to send them out for spiritual warfare in the world outside the

church offices, but to do nothing themselves about outreach (I personally know
several pastors of megachurches who consistently visit people and witness to them
explaining, "We as pastors and church
staffers should never ask our members to
do what we won't do").

• An entrenched lay leadership that
defends "the way we were" and the status
quo, and often vehemently refuses to move
out into the community with the compassion of their supposed Lord.

• A pervasive spirit of "live and let live,"
"don't rock the boat," "they know where the
church is, so let 'em find it," "those sinners
made their bed, so let 'em lie in it," and so on.

Tragically, many of these stagnant or dying churches
have lost their vision. "Where there is no vision, the people
perish" (Proverbs 29:18). The members often pray and testify, "Our church is a light on the hilltop" when it is perhaps
a darkness "down in the valley, valley so low." All too many
of the church's leaders may be neglecting their responsibility to submit to Christ's Lordship, instead becoming
ecclesiastical "lords" unto themselves, sitting in judgment
not only on the unchurched but often on the churched,
especially those new members who are struggling to become victorious believers (often without sufficient counseling and follow-up).

Let a relatively new convert start missing the services
and showing signs of drifting, and, instead of being available to lovingly counsel and/or visit that person, members
or even leaders will sometimes make snide comments such
as, "Well, I knew he wouldn't last." "She's a member now
and knows her responsibilities, so I don't see why we have
to concern ourselves about her." "He probably never was

saved in the first place." Because no effort is made to contact the person, he or she assumes the church doesn't care (which, unfortunately, is true in these cases). It's this kind of lack of concern for people that can easily end up turning people away from God rather than toward Him.

Cornelius Platinga, Jr., in his article, "Natural Born Sinners," incisively laid the "typical" Christian's and church's problem on the line:

> Some of us retreat into the small world defined by our friends, work, church, and family and build a snuggery there. Inside it, we may be busy enough, but with only local concerns. Perhaps on television we watch with disdain or amazement the passing show of misery, novelty, and grief in the larger world outside, but if our insulation is good enough, we need not be disturbed and, in any case, we do not wish to be inconvenienced....We dismiss the needs of future generations. We have never dealt seriously with a homeless person. We do not grieve over news stories of poverty or starvation, and we make only token efforts to relieve such suffering by our charity. Claiming allegiance to the Christ who speaks in active imperatives (Go! Tell! Witness! Declare! Proclaim!), we Christians nonetheless prefer to keep the Bread of Life in our own cupboard and to speak of it only to those who already have it. Do we, perhaps, subconsciously suppose that in such inbred silence we can keep our dignity and unbelievers can go to hell where they belong?[4]

ARE WE LIKE JESUS?

E. Stanley Jones, a foreign missionary with a tremendous passion for bringing people to Christ, was pleading with a group of young people in India.

> "I wish you would stand up and tell me, if you will, why you are not Christians. Why will you not become Christians? What do you think of Christ? Why will you not follow Him?" Then one young Indian answered, "Your Christ is wonderful, but you Christians are not like Him."[5]

Through the history of Christianity, I wonder how many millions of times unsaved people have given that answer in one form or another. What do the lost of your community think and speak about you as an individual and your church collectively? What the lost world thinks of you and your church makes this difference: If you are uncaring and insensitive, thus betraying the compassionate Christ, people are likely not to receive the Lord and Savior you claim to proclaim.

No characteristic more epitomizes the Lord Jesus than compassion.

> Jesus went through all the towns and villages, teaching in their synagogues, preaching the good news of the kingdom and healing every disease and sickness. When he saw the crowds, he had compassion on them, because they were harassed and helpless ["fainted, and were scattered abroad," KJV], like sheep without a shepherd (Matthew 9:35-36 NIV).

Yet Jesus also sternly scolded the self-righteous scribes and Pharisees who constantly opposed Him and tried to trap Him by asking controversial questions concerning Roman and Jewish law. He vitriolically referred to them as "hypocrites," "blind guides," and "fools"; those who scrupulously tithed but overlooked the "weightier matters of the law, judgment, mercy, and faith"; those who would "strain at a gnat and swallow a camel"; those who were "full of extortion and excess"; "whited sepulchers which indeed appear beautiful outward, but are within full of dead men's bones, and of all uncleanness"; "full of hypocrisy and iniquity," "children of them which killed the prophets," "serpents" who could not "escape the damnation of hell"; those guilty of "all the righteous blood shed upon the earth, from the blood of righteous Abel" to the blood of a fellow named Zacharias, whom they had recently killed between the temple and the altar (see Matthew 23:13-35). Whew! With such strong indictments, we can understand why those religious leaders wanted to kill Jesus!

A VIVID CONTRAST

Jesus was loving and tender toward those who sought His forgiveness, admitted their sins, and repented. Recall the woman caught in the act of adultery (see John 8:1-11). The religious leaders, with rocks already in hand, were ready to stone her into eternity with their missiles of self-righteousness.

After our compassionate Lord stooped and wrote in the sand (most likely He was listing the sins of the religious leaders), and all her accusers had departed like sidewinder rattlesnakes, He asked, "Woman, where are those thine accusers? Hath no man condemned thee?" (John 8:10), to which she replied, "No man, Lord" (verse 11). The passage closes on an exhilarating note: "Neither do I condemn thee: go, and sin no more" (verse 11). To all of us who are saved, Jesus has spoken within the deepest recesses of our hearts, souls, and spirits, "Neither do I condemn thee: go, and sin no more."

And what about the woman at the well (John 4:6-24)? Without any prior investigation, Jesus plainly stated, "You are right when you say you have no husband. The fact is, you have had five husbands, and the man you now have is not your husband. What you have just said is quite true" (verses 17-18 NIV). By the time the conversation had ended, the woman was convinced that Jesus was the long-awaited Messiah and immediately dashed into town to share the news with others.

Then there was the thief on the cross who cried, "Lord, remember me when thou comest into thy kingdom" (Luke 23:42). And the loving Lord, in His agony, answered, "Today shalt thou be with me in paradise" (verse 43).

In every one of those instances (and many more), Jesus reached out to the undesirables—the castoffs of society. These people were clearly sinners, but that didn't keep our Lord from ministering to them. Are we avoiding the unlovables, the rejects? Do we see the lost as Christ saw them—as souls searching for the love, care, and fulfillment that only He can provide? Jesus preached firmly against sin, but He did so with a heart of compassion. Likewise, we ought to proclaim the horrible consequences of sin, but we ought to do it with hearts that are breaking for lost souls. We must have the kindness and mercy of our Lord Jesus, who was "moved with compassion" on the multitude because they "fainted, and were scattered abroad, as sheep having no shepherd" (Matthew 9:36).

A POWERFUL EXAMPLE

Anita Bryant is an example to us of taking a stand against sin yet ministering with compassion:

> ...Anita Bryant had it all. She had
> recorded 30 albums, written 10 books and

had the Florida Citrus Commission contract. Three times she had been voted *Good
Housekeeping's* Most Admired Woman. She
did 14 command performances at the
White House, sang at the funeral of President Lyndon Johnson, and traveled on
seven consecutive Bob Hope Christmas
tours....Her stand against the homosexual
rights movement resulted in a gay backlash
that caused her world to cave in. She lost
contracts for 80 conventions where she was
to perform as well as the lucrative orange
juice promotion contract. She went through
a bitter and public divorce in 1980.[6]

Anita, after suffering every sort of demeaning insult
and obscene indignity from homosexuals, also had a shocking number of Christians boycott her and turn against her.
Several years after taking her stand against preferential
treatment for homosexuals, she began rebuilding her
career as a singer-entertainer, and in her ministry she
included witnessing to homosexuals. In her book *A New
Day*, in which she writes about her comeback, she wrote
compassionately about her visits to an AIDS patient named
Ken, who responded by accepting Christ. She testified in
that book:

> Having experienced such criticism,
> ridicule, and hatred, I suppose I'll always
> feel compassion for others in that situation,
> regardless of whether they seem to deserve
> such fallout. The fact is, I've received in full
> measure the compassion and forgiveness of
> my Lord Jesus Christ. How can I offer my
> hurting brother or sister anything less?[7]

Anita is living out the kindness and compassion of her Lord, which is every Christian's and every church's divine commission from their Redeemer. How do we, as Anita did, cultivate the compassion of Christ?

First, we must never forget that, at one time, we were "dead in [our] trespasses and sins" (see Ephesians 2:1). Even in that condition, the Lord and Savior Jesus Christ reached out to us in kindness and tenderness. And we, in turn, are to demonstrate, in word and deed, the *agape* love that we have received from Him.

Second, we must pray for His compassion to permeate our lives and overflow to all those around us, not only to the "*down* and outs" but also to the "*up* and outs." Isaiah prophesied of the compassion that would mark Jesus long before the Savior was ever born:

> Behold my servant, whom I uphold: mine elect, in whom my soul delighteth; I have put my spirit upon him: he shall bring forth judgment to the Gentiles....A bruised reed shall he not break, and the smoking flax shall he not quench: he shall bring forth judgment unto truth (42:1,3).

According to Isaiah, Jesus would be so kind, gentle, and tender that even though He would bring "forth judgment unto truth," He would not even trample the crushed reed or papyrus that grew along the riverbank. Neither would he snuff out the barely burning wick, or flax, of an oil lamp.

Is that the kind of compassion that characterizes your life? Our prayer should be this: "Lord, help me to view fellow believers and the desperately lost world through the tear-filled eyes of Jesus, who wept not only for Jerusalem and Lazarus, but for all humanity."

Let us revive that touching hymn, "The Great Physician":

The Great Physician now is near,
The sympathizing Jesus;
He speaks the drooping heart to cheer,
Oh! hear the voice of Jesus.
Sweetest note in seraph song,
Sweetest name on mortal tongue;
Sweetest carol ever sung,
Jesus, blessed Jesus.

—William Hunter

— 6 —

A Bible
Without Trust

And so, I thought, the anvil of God's Word
For ages the skeptics' blows have beat upon,
But through the noise of falling blows was heard
The anvil is unchanged; the hammers gone.
                                    —John Clifford

Don J. Gutteridge, Jr., in his book entitled *The Defense Rests Its Case*, wrote: "Probably the most frequently asked question in Christian and non-Christian circles is, 'Is the Bible really the Word of God, and is it reliable?'" [1]

The matrix of this entire book is the Bible, God's objective written revelation of His redemptive plan for earth's inhabitants (see 2 Timothy 3:16-17; John 1:1-3,14). If we fail to adhere to biblical truth, then we will not have a clear-cut sense of God's intervention in the affairs of human-kind. And worse, we will have an inadequate perception of Christ, a problem we examined in the previous chapter.

Dr. W. A. Criswell, pastor emeritus of First Baptist Church, Dallas, ably articulated the interrelationship of the living Word, Christ, and the written Word, God's Book:

The written word, the spoken word, the incarnate word are all three inseparably tied together. God is identified with His Word, and the Word is identified with God—the written Word, the spoken Word, and the incarnate Word. Whenever I receive the Word of God, I receive God Himself. When I believe the Word of God, I believe God Himself. Spiritually, when I know the Word of God, I trust God Himself. When I trust the Word of God, I trust God Himself. God and His Word are identified forever. The Psalmist says, "For ever, O Lord, thy word is settled in heaven" (Psalm 119:89). God's Word is like God Himself, the same yesterday, today, and forever.[2]

ABANDONING THE BIBLE

It astounds me that appreciable numbers of professing Christians believe and teach that the Bible is a good book yet is not completely adequate for contemporary society and assuredly not trustworthy in matters outside of spiritual truth. Then there are those who go so far as to futilely endeavor to restructure and rewrite the Bible.

Sad to say, there are many churches and ministers that hold to the view that the Bible is an archaic, out-of-touch book. They have fallen prey to Satan's question in the Garden of Eden, "Indeed, has God said...?" (Genesis 3:1 NASB). In all the subsequent centuries Satan's tactic has not changed; his favorite strategy is to foment doubt about the authority of God's Word, whether spoken or written.

So many who attempt to compartmentalize the Book, claiming it is dependable in part but not as a whole, also adhere to faulty theories, not only about the Bible but also concerning the origin of mankind and the meaning of salvation. Some of these same people advocate the theory of evolution as though it were a religious dogma and is totally irrefutable. Even if they profess to believe in God's creation, they accommodate themselves by contending that God used evolution as the means of propagating the human race, and that people have evolved for perhaps millions of years from lower forms of life. These individuals find it hard to take the Bible at face value—to simply believe exactly what it says about God's instantaneous work of creation.

There are seemingly well-meaning Christians who emphatically state, "We must judge the Bible in the light of Jesus Christ," yet they don't uphold the Bible in its entirety. That's unfortunate because everything we could ever know about Christ is found in the Bible. If we cannot depend on the Bible and trust its authority, then we are going to hurt our perception of Jesus and are going to cut ourselves adrift without moorings.

No Bible, no Jesus. You can't undermine one without undermining the other. After all, how do we know about Jesus? *The Bible.* How do we know about the Father and the Spirit, the other persons of the Trinity? *The Bible.* How do we gain insight into mankind's sinful, unregenerate condition and God's corresponding provision for our salvation? *The Bible.*

CONTENDING FOR THE FAITH

Apologetics is the study of the evidence for and the validity of the Christian faith. Some preachers and professors dismiss apologetics and say, "The Bible doesn't need defending. We simply must preach it," but that is an inadequate stance to take in this day of widespread departure from the Bible as a standard for personal and national ethics and morality. Scripture affirms that we need to be ready to defend our faith. We are instructed by Jude:

> Beloved, when I gave all diligence to write unto you of the common salvation, it was needful for me to write unto you, and exhort you that ye should earnestly contend for the faith [the Christian body of truth] which was once delivered unto the saints (verse 3).

Are you prepared to give an answer for "the hope that is in you"? (1 Peter 3:15). If you have doubts about and trouble with the inerrancy and infallibility of God's Word, this following section is particularly for you.

PROOFS IN SUPPORT OF THE BIBLE

The Bible Verifies Itself

One potent proof of the Bible's authority is that it verifies itself. Critics of the Bible such as James Barr have made irresponsible statements like this:

> According to conservative arguments… the Bible…"claims" to be divinely inspired. All this is nonsense. There is no "the Bible" that claims to be divinely inspired, there is no "it" that has a "view of itself." There is only this or that source, like 2 Timothy or 2 Peter, which makes statements about certain other writings, these rather undefined. There is no such thing as "the Bible's view of itself" from which a fully authoritative answer to these questions can be obtained.[3]

Such a vacuous passage hardly calls for an answer. How can anyone read the Bible and not immediately recognize that it repeatedly refers to itself as the very words of God, collectively "the Word of God," drawn together over a period of about 1,500 years? One prophet after another asserted, "The word of the Lord came unto me" (see, for example, Hosea 1:1; Joel 1:1; Zephaniah 1:1). The prophet Jeremiah said, "The LORD put forth his hand, and touched my mouth. And the LORD said unto me, Behold, I have put my words in thy mouth" (Jeremiah 1:9).

Longtime Bible teacher W.A. Criswell said this:

> With complete and perfect assurance I can pick up my Bible and know that I read the revealed Word of God. The God who inspired it also took faithful care that it be exactly preserved through the fire and the blood of the centuries....The same blessed *Paraclete*, the Holy Spirit of God, who brought to the remembrance of the disciples the spoken Word of Jesus that it might become indelible in the written Word, also preserved the sacred writing from mutilation and destruction.[4]

Both the Old and New Testaments again and again refer to themselves as being the words of God (see 1 Kings 22:8-16; Nehemiah 8; Psalm 119; Romans 3:2; 1 Peter 1:10-12). God either spoke directly to His people or through His prophets and messengers:

> The prophecy came not in old time by the will of man: but holy men of God spake as they were moved by the Holy Ghost (2 Peter 1:21 KJV).

> Thus, the Bible insists that God not only addresses humankind universally through nature, history, and the reason and conscience of men and women but also addresses His word to and through certain

persons in special ways. Over and over again, God is identified as a speaking God who reveals His message to a specific individual in a unique place at a particular time.[5]

Jesus' Testimony About the Bible

The number-one proof of the Scriptures' validity is the testimony of Jesus Christ Himself. Jesus believed and taught the law and the prophets of the Old Testament. In certain places He authenticated them, but in numerous cases He expanded on them, as He did in the Sermon on the Mount and other teachings.

During His temptation in the wilderness, Jesus withstood the onslaught of the devil by answering each of the three satanic challenges with the words: "It is written..."—all from the book of Deuteronomy (8:3, 6:16, 6:13—compare with Matthew 4:1-11).

In John 10:35, Jesus declared to the Jewish religious leaders that the Scripture cannot be broken. One Bible scholar made this observation:

> Jesus Christ binds and unites everything in Scripture—beginning and end, creation and redemption, humanity, the fall, history, and the future. If this overriding unity is neglected, Scripture can become denatured, losing its "theological-Christological definition" and becoming abstracted from the peculiar nature and content of Scripture.[6]

The Testaments Verify One Another

Another pivotal proof of the Bible's dependability and veracity is that the New Testament verifies the Old, and the Old verifies the New. When Paul preached and wrote about Jesus Christ, more than likely none of the Gospels were yet in circulation, perhaps with the exception of Mark. Paul predicated his gospel message on the Old Testament. In his writings and the other books of the New Testament we find quotations from and allusions to Genesis, Exodus, Deuteronomy, Numbers, Joshua, Judges, 1 and 2 Samuel, 1 Kings, 1 Chronicles, Psalms, Isaiah, Job, Amos, Jeremiah, Ezekiel, Micah, Zechariah, Daniel, Hosea, and Habakkuk.

Westcott and Hort's classic *Greek New Testament* indicates that there are 74 Old Testament quotations in Romans, 29 in 1 Corinthians, 13 in Galatians, and 21 in Ephesians. Study on my own has revealed at least 34 probable allusions to Old Testament passages in 2 Corinthians, 24 in Philippians, 12 in Colossians, 18 in 1 Thessalonians, 13 in 2 Thessalonians, 20 in 1 Timothy, 19 in 2 Timothy, four in Titus, and one in Philemon.

There is disagreement today over who God used to write the book of Hebrews; my personal feeling is that Paul wrote it. In addition to its overriding Jewish tone, the book of Hebrews contains at least 140 references to the Old Testament! To have so many references would require someone who knew the Old Testament well, for the writer most likely could not have carried a copy of the Scriptures with him on his journeys because the scrolls would have been so large and heavy.

The Bible's Persistence

Another profound evidence of the Bible's authenticity is that it has survived in the most marvelous way in spite of being so consistently hated and opposed through the centuries. Two hundred years ago Francois Voltaire, the blatant French atheist, proclaimed, "Within 100 years the Bible will have disappeared from the face of the earth....Ere the beginnings of the nineteenth century Christianity will have perished from the earth....If we would destroy the Christian religion, we must first of all destroy man's belief in the Bible."

It is remarkable that for decades after his horrific death—during which he screamed, "O, the terrors of the damned!"—the Geneva (Switzerland) Bible Society printed its Bibles on the very press where Voltaire had turned out copies of his disproved prophecy. Voltaire is long gone, but the Bible, the Word of God, will continue and abide forever.

No similarly lengthy campaigns of bitter condemnation and destruction have been waged against other major religious works, such as the Hindu and Muslim "holy books," the Koran and the Gitas, and the Book of Mormon that the Latter-day Saints revere above the Bible. Tyrants through the centuries—such as Hitler, Stalin, Mao Tse-tung, and other Muslim, Fascist, and Communist totalitarian despots all over the world—have directed massive Bible burnings and conscriptions, oftentimes imprisoning or murdering owners of the Scriptures. In many nations where Buddhism, Hinduism, or Islam are the state religions, owning a Bible and professing faith in Christ can mean death. Such persecution is not merely a relic of the past; it is actually on the rise as we enter the twenty-first century.

In ages past, translators and distributors of God's Word—like William Tyndale and John Wycliffe—were tortured, strangled, and burned at the stake by the hands or orders of state-church inquisitors who believed the Scriptures were only for priests and higher-ups in a hierarchy. For centuries the Bible was kept locked and chained in cathedrals. The common people had no access to the Holy Writ; all they knew was whatever they were taught by church officials, who were considered the sole agents of God's truth.

In the sixteenth century William Tyndale, the English reformer and martyr, affirmed, "If God spare my life, I will cause a boy that driveth the plow to know more of the Scripture than thou [a learned man] dost." Tyndale finished his translation secretly in exile. When the completed translation was smuggled into England, copies were burned by order of the Bishop of London.

Tyndale was working on his translation of the Old Testament at Antwerp (Belgium) when an agent of England's King Henry VIII ratted on the translator. Tyndale was arrested and sent to prison, where he languished for two years.

The king, known for either beheading or divorcing his wives, insisted on Tyndale's execution. In 1536 Tyndale was chained to a stake, strangled, and then burned. His last words were, "Lord, open the king of England's eyes." It is extraordinary that the year after his martyrdom the Bible was published throughout England by the command of that very king and was appointed to be read by all the people!

The Bible's Truthfulness

Another unusual proof that the Bible is God's inerrant, infallible Word is that it doesn't hide the flaws in the lives of its heroes and heroines. In generations past, we usually heard nothing but good about our political and religious leaders. Seldom did we hear criticisms about their flaws and sins. It was a common human quality to overlook the faults of those we respected.

For example, Franklin Delano Roosevelt—who was elected to four terms—could do no wrong for most Americans. Today, however, many years after his death, his faults are being exposed. That was also true of army general Dwight David Eisenhower, our supreme commander in Europe during World War II and our president from 1952-1960. During those years, people admired him, tending to gloss over any weaknesses he had. But now people look back and, though they still respect him, they also know he wasn't bigger-than-life.

While people today are much more candid about the flaws of leaders and the famous, still, there is an inclination to dismiss the flaws as being inconsequential or irrelevant.

By contrast, the Bible doesn't try to hide people's character flaws. You would have thought that modern-day investigative journalists were hot on the trail of luminaries like Noah, Abraham, Isaac, Jacob, Joseph, Moses, David, Paul, Peter, and many more. Although they were shining stars for God, they often plummeted—lying, becoming drunk, committing adultery, cheating, stealing, and even cursing God and denying their relationship to Him. The Bible's candor is another proof of its inspiration.

The Bible's Ability to Change Lives

Another confirmation of the Bible's validity is the revolutionary change it makes in human lives. Scripture's ethical and moral standards are unparalleled. Adherence to the principles of the Word and receiving the Christ revealed in the Bible has turned even the worst of sinners into wonderful Christians. Prostitutes, homosexuals, and murderers have come to know real change through the Bible—going from lives of immorality, debauchery, and hatred to purity, virtue, and love.

John Newton, once a greedy, degenerate trafficker in slaves, received Christ as His Savior and testified, "Christ transformed this wild beast." Newton is best known as the writer of probably the most-beloved hymn of modern times, "Amazing Grace."

Ted Bundy, the notorious serial killer of maybe 60 or more young women, prior to his execution in Florida, supposedly accepted Jesus. Shortly before his death Bundy was interviewed by Christian radio host and author James Dobson. Bundy expressed profound grief over his bloody crimes, confessing the role pornography had played in his monstrous aberrations and testifying to his newfound faith in Christ. If he were truly sincere, the one-time cold-blooded murderer, cleansed by Christ's blood, is in heaven today...believe it or not. Yes, the grace of the Christ found on the sacred pages of the Bible is amazing!

The Bible's Support from Archaeology

Another powerful validation of the Bible is the findings of archaeology. Beginning in the late eighteenth century, archaeologists, both Christian and non-Christian, began digging for artifacts in the Bible lands. In the years since, a wealth of evidence has been found that supports the Bible's truthfulness. For instance, Lachish, Debir, and Hazor (see Joshua 10:31-38; 11:1) were at one time considered fictitious towns, but all have been uncovered, thus proving the accuracy of the Bible's historical accounts.

Still other biblical facts have been vindicated. We have discovered either direct or indirect evidence of Jericho and Ai, of Sodom and Gomorrah, of the Hittites and many other Canaanite tribes. For years cynics thought the Hittites had never existed, but archaeology has confirmed that they were a real people.

Edward P. Blair, in his *Abingdon Bible Handbook*, outlined archaeology in this manner: a. The Bible Guides the Work of Archaeologists; b. Archaeology Uncovers Places and Objects Mentioned in the Bible; c. Archaeology Supplements and Explains Many Biblical Dates; d. Archaeology Probes the Bible; e. Archaeology Confirms the Bible; and f. Archaeology Reveals the Uniqueness of the Judeo-Christian Religion and Literature.[7] While I do not agree with all of his conclusions, Blair cites significant facts about how archaeology has affirmed the Bible's documentation of the events, persons, and living conditions found in the Middle East during Bible times.

Dr. Nelson Glueck, an outstanding Jewish archaeologist, wrote, "It may be stated categorically that no archaeological discovery has ever controverted a biblical reference."[8]

The Bible and Fulfilled Prophecies

Finally, the many fulfilled prophecies regarding the Messiah provides major support for *proof of the Bible's validity*. Jesus emphasized, "Do not think that I came to abolish the Law or the Prophets; I did not come to abolish, but to fulfill" (Matthew 5:17 NASB). According to various authors there are between 300 to 1,000 Messianic prophecies in the Old Testament. Don Gutteridge set forth ten major prophecies concerning the life and mission of the Lord Jesus:

1. *Born of a virgin*
   Prophecy: Isaiah 7:14 NASB
   Fulfillment: Matthew 1:18 TLB
2. *Born in Bethlehem*
   Prophecy: Micah 5:2 TLB
   Fulfillment: Matthew 2:1 TLB
3. *Betrayed for 30 pieces of silver*
   Prophecy: Zechariah 11:12 TLB
   Fulfillment: Matthew 26:15 TLB
4. *Beat and spat upon*
   Prophecy: Isaiah 50:6 TLB
   Fulfillment: Matthew 26:67 TLB
5. *Hands and feet pierced*
   Prophecy: Psalm 22:16 TLB
   Fulfillment: Luke 23:33 TLB
6. *Crucified with thieves*
   Prophecy: Isaiah 53:12 TLB
   Fulfillment: Matthew 27:38 TLB
7. *Gambled for His clothes*
   Prophecy: Psalm 22:18
   Fulfillment: John 19:23-24 TLB
8. *Bones were not broken*
   Prophecy: Psalm 34:20 KJV
   Fulfillment: John 19:33 NASB
9. *His side pierced*
   Prophecy: Zechariah 12:10 TLB
   Fulfillment: John 19:34 TLB

10. *Buried in a rich man's tomb*
    Prophecy: Isaiah 53:9 TLB
    Fulfillment: Matthew 27:57-60 TLB [9]

A BOOK WE CAN TRUST

Indeed, we have every reason to trust the Bible. There is nothing else upon which we can stand so firmly. It is a sure foundation that will never change, never crumble. Kingdoms will come and go; people will waver to and fro. But the Bible is absolutely steadfast. It is worthy of our trust. It is wholly adequate for our every need. There is no reason for us to ever doubt it or question it.

It all boils down to these crucial questions: Do you trust Jesus Christ and have faith in Him and His words? Do you believe the record that God has given us of redemptive history to the extent that you are prepared to face a skeptical world and unashamedly share the Living Word and His written Word?

John closed his Gospel with these words of supreme confidence:

> *These are written, that ye might believe that Jesus is the Christ, the Son of God; and that believing ye might have life through his name* (John 20:31).

— 7 —

A Christ
Without Distinction

*To recognize that half of all the people who
accept the biblical account of Jesus' death, resurrection and eternal life nevertheless have not
sought any type of serious, permanent relationship with Him is rather astonishing. This must
raise some questions both about our culture and
the ways the American church fosters its faith
within the context of this culture. As well, a
majority of unchurched adults (64%) and non-
Christians (77%) assert that He died, rose and
exists today.*[1]

—George Barna

Two millennia after Jesus' incarnation, it seems that the
majority of people even in the Western world still have no
concept of who this Jesus, the Christ, is. Sad to say, the only
time many individuals hear His name is when it is used as
part of a profane epithet.

REINVENTING JESUS

Perhaps you have heard of the "Jesus Seminar"—a
group of liberal, "free-thinking" scholars who gather once

a year in an attempt to recreate and redefine the person of Jesus. This small band of so-called intelligentsia claims that most of the words attributed to Him in the New Testament are not His own, and that Jesus never really said that He was God. In fact, some members of the Jesus Seminar claim He exists only as a figment of the imagination.

Even though the major matters concerning the character and person of Christ were decided and settled by Christian councils by the fourth century A.D., through the ages there have been those who have attested that Jesus was nothing more than a mere man, a clever rabbi, or even a false prophet.

Liberal theologian Nels Ferre, in his book *The Sun and the Umbrella*, wrote that Jesus may have been the offspring of a blonde Roman soldier and a Jewish harlot. Among other things, people have argued that Jesus Christ is no more authoritative than other well-known teachers, such as Lao-tse, Confucius, Buddha, Zoroaster, Socrates, Plato, or Aristotle. All of these perspectives and opinions have endeavored to erode the credibility of God's objective written revelation, the Bible, and the leading of the Holy Spirit, without whom there is neither salvation nor our inward verification of the validity of the sacred Scriptures.

Jesus, John, Paul, and Peter all prophesied that scoffers and antichrists would arise. As we approach the last days these false prophets will multiply. While these teachers say that they base their foundation on the Bible, they also express doubts about its authenticity or twist its content in an attempt to prove perverted points. You may hear them admit, "We accept certain portions of the Bible but not all of it, and we have problems with accepting the historic Jesus. He was generally a good man, but He has been idealized by religious fanatics and made into something more than He really was."

How tragic it is that multitudes of people still either try to dispose of Jesus or reinvent Him. He entered this world expressly to reveal Himself as God, as the Son of God, as the Savior of all those who would call on Him, and as the embodiment of all God's truth incarnate in the perfect combination of humanity and deity, yet without sin. John tells us that "He came unto His own, and his own received Him not, but as many as received him, to them gave He power to become the sons of God" (John 1:11-12).

WHO DO YOU SAY I AM?

The Testimony of Men

Throughout Jesus' earthly ministry and in subsequent centuries, all stripes of people have asked, "Jesus, who are You?" The scribes and Pharisees, the Romans, and the Gentiles grappled with that question. All across the globe, people are still asking that piercing question.

At one point in His ministry, Jesus asked His disciples, "Whom do men say that I the Son of man am? And they said, Some say that thou art John the Baptist: some, Elijah; and others, Jeremiah, or one of the prophets" (Matthew 16:13-14).

Those answers were not correct, and it's possible the disciples might have thought they were rather complimentary. But notice what happened next:

> He saith unto them, But whom say ye that I am? And Simon Peter answered and said, Thou art the Christ, the Son of the living God. And Jesus answered and said unto him, Blessed art thou, Simon Bar-jona: for flesh and blood hath not revealed it unto thee, but my Father which is in heaven (Matthew 16:16-17).

The Testimony of Jesus

Jesus was very specific about Himself in John 14:6:

> I am the way, the truth, and the life: no man cometh unto the Father, but by me.

If Jesus' claim was not factual, then it was one of the most brazen claims by any religious teacher, preacher, or philosopher who ever lived. If He were not the way, the truth, and the life, then He was either a congenital liar or a madman.

But Jesus was candid and consistent. Not once did He ever deny the claims that He was God and that He was the "only begotten Son of God." When people asked if He was God, He often replied, in essence, "You said it." So those who claim that Jesus did not recognize His deity apparently refuse to accept the New Testament accounts because they clearly show that Jesus knew who He was.

If Jesus were merely an honest rabbinical teacher and not a madman, then He never would have allowed people to call Him the Son of God or the Son of David, because Scripture reveals the Son of David to be the Messiah promised in the Old Testament. That leaves us with two choices: Either Jesus really was the Son of God, or He was a liar.

Bible teacher G. Campbell Morgan wrote:

> He [Jesus] was the God-man. Not God indwelling a man. Of such there have been many. Not a man deified. Of such there have been none save in the myths of pagan systems of thought; but God and man, combining in one Personality the two natures, a perpetual enigma and mystery, baffling the possibility of explanation.[2]

THE INSANITY CONTINUES

In spite of the clear teaching of God's Word, there are those who still set out on what they call "the quest for the historical Jesus." Here are some books that came out in time for the Christmas season one year:

The Historical Figure of Jesus by E. P. Sanders. Atheists might argue Jesus never existed. Sanders says the evidence from a historian's viewpoint is overwhelming that He did. But questions like "What was He really like?" and "What did He think about himself?" can be answered only in probabilities, not certainties....[3]

Jesus: A Revolutionary Biography by J. D. Crossan. To this amiable, liberal Catholic scholar, Jesus and his followers were Galilean "hippies in a world of Augustan yuppies." ...Crossan uses the *Gospel of Thomas* (discovered in Egypt in 1945) as a source for Jesus' teachings along with the four biblical gospel books.[4]

Jesus: Miriam's Child, Sophia's Prophet by Elizabeth Schussler Florenza. A groundbreaking feminist expert argues that Jesus was a messenger of Divine Sophia, or Woman Wisdom, a powerful figure from early Jewish tradition. After his death Jesus' vision of universal justice was destroyed by male-dominated leaders.[5]

Incidentally, the extreme feminists' Sophia movement reached an incredible low with the "Re-imagining Conference" at Minneapolis in 1994, in which "Sophia," a female goddess—instead of God the Father and Jesus the Son—was praised and worshiped. In addition, the program included a praise service by avowed lesbians.

Susan Cyre in *Christianity Today* reported about the "Goddess" Sophia worship at the conference:

Working from a basis in feminist theology, conference participants looked to pantheistic religions and the heretical Gnostic gospels to "reimagine" a new god and a new road to salvation. The attendees blessed, thanked, and praised Sophia as a deity. Organizers claimed Sophia is the embodiment of wisdom, found in the first nine chapters of Proverbs. Sophia, they said, was with God at the Creation, and she is "the tree of life to those who lay hold of her...."[6]

"I can no longer worship in a theological context that depicts God as an abusive parent and Jesus as the obedient, trusting child," Virginia Mollenkott said. "This violent theology encourages the violence of our streets and nation....

Feminist theologian Delores Williams, referring to the Atonement, said: "I don't think we need folks hanging on crosses and blood dripping and weird stuff." Chinese feminist Kwok Pui-Lan claimed, "If we cannot imagine Jesus as a tree, as a river, as wind, and as rain, we are doomed together." Korean university professor Chung Hyun Kyung led the group in trying to harness the divine energy of the universe using New Age techniques....

As an apparent substitute for the Lord's Supper, leaders said, "Sophia, we celebrate the nourishment of your milk and honey" in an invitation to "the banquet table of Creation."[7]

Thank God for leaders like retired United Methodist Church bishops Earl Hunt and Mack B. Stokes—Hunt forthrightly declared that "no comparable heresy has appeared in the church in the last 15 centuries." Stokes called the conference "theologically ignorant...ontologically superstitious...Christologically blasphemous...ecclesiastically irresponsible."[8]

THE SOURCES OF THIS CONFUSION

So-Called Christian Educational Institutions

How is this sort of heresy perpetuated? Ultimately it's the deceiver, the devil, who is behind all this. He is the father of lies and the author of all confusion and untruth (John 8:44). But on the human level, one source of these teachings is, amazingly enough, Christian colleges and seminaries. Time and again I've encountered young people who have gone off to college or seminary, often spiritually aflame for God and bursting with biblical knowledge, only to have their zeal and learning quenched as they hear from a professor that Jesus was only human and that the Bible is not inspired but merely a unique collection of Oriental writings.

If these students ever had saving faith, they will not lose their salvation, but they can certainly become confused and sidetracked. The errant teaching from their professors is like a polluted stream that courses into otherwise pure water and spreads its toxicity. Such unbiblical teaching is often excused as an expression of "academic freedom."

Christian writer Chuck Swindoll has observed that knowledge alone can be dangerous, emphasizing four perils of misinformed, misguided knowledge:

> 1. Knowledge can be dangerous when it lacks scriptural support—intelligent, biblical support....
> 2. Knowledge can be dangerous when it becomes an end in itself....

3. Knowledge can be dangerous when it isn't balanced by love and grace....

4. Knowledge can be dangerous when it remains theoretical—when it isn't mixed with discernment and action.[9]

Even though my own denomination, the Southern Baptist Convention, emphasizes that its only creed is the Word of God, the convention has found it essential to prepare a doctrinal statement called "The Baptist Faith and Message" (first adopted in 1925 and revised in 1963), which rather positively articulates what Baptists have basically believed through the centuries. Our seminaries have articles of faith that every professor must sign and concur with if he or she wants to teach in our theological institutions.

It's interesting to note that Christian colleges and seminaries that allow "anything goes" teaching in their classrooms have continued to decline over the years, sending forth doubting, questioning, and even unbelieving ministers, church leaders, and church staff members. Some time ago one of my friends ate lunch with an outstanding pastor-evangelist from a certain mainline denomination. My friend reported that the great preacher—one of a dying breed in his disintegrating denomination—was overcome with emotion and tears as he confessed, "It hurts so bad. Our denomination doesn't have a foreign missions program anymore because most all of our leaders believe Buddhism, Hinduism, and Islam are about as good as Christianity."

Cult Groups

Christian colleges and seminaries aren't the only culprits in the spread of half-truths and deceptive teachings. Cults have done tremendous damage as well. They claim to point people to God, but their teachings do anything but that. Think of David Koresh and his Branch Davidians, Jim Jones and his Guyana cult, and Reverend Moon and his devotees. They represent more extreme factions in the cult world; unfortunately, there are also cults that give the appearance of being a part of mainstream Christianity because they profess to adhere to God's Word.

Why are cults able to attract so many followers? Swindoll tells us:

> False teachers have no qualms about leading people into the realm of error. They're convinced that what they are teaching is true. Along with an abundance of charisma, they have the ability to persuade others to buy into their position. And they have what they call "facts" to pull you away from where you stand. Again, this is not some superficial scare tactic from a wide-eyed fanatic…it is true. Remember the Spirit *explicitly* warns of such.[10]

Established Churches

Finally, throughout Christian history, stalwart believers have had to contend with false teachers in the churches. It started in the New Testament era with the Judaizers or Galatianists (those who believed a Gentile must first become a proselyte Jew before he could become a Christian), the Antinomians (who were libertines and swung in the opposite direction from the Judaizers), and the Gnostics (who had extremely flawed views of Jesus' nature).

The apostle Paul frequently warned against false teachers and teachings in the church. For example, in Galatians 1:8-9 he said:

> Though we, or an angel from heaven, preach any other gospel unto you than that which we have preached unto you, let him

be accursed. As we said before, so say I now again, If any man preach any other gospel unto you than that ye have received, let him be accursed.

If I am not mistaken, this is the only place in all of Paul's epistles where he repeats himself in such a manner. It's as though he is saying, "I've told you once, and now I'm telling you again."

In both 1 and 2 Timothy, Paul again sounded warnings:

Now the Spirit speaketh expressly, that in the latter times some shall depart from the faith, giving heed to seducing spirits, and doctrines of devils; speaking lies in hypocrisy; having their conscience seared with a hot iron....If thou put the brethren in remembrance of these things, thou shalt be a good minister of Jesus Christ, nourished up in the words of faith and of good doctrine, whereunto thou hast attained.... Take heed unto thyself, and unto the doctrine; continue in them: for in doing this thou shalt both save thyself, and them that hear thee (1 Timothy 4:1-2,6,16).

The time will come when they will not endure sound doctrine; but after their own lusts shall they heap to themselves teachers, having itching ears; and they shall turn away their ears from the truth, and shall be turned unto fables (2 Timothy 4:3-4).

In his epistles, Paul repeatedly stressed the significance of sound doctrine—solid, substantial teaching concerning Christ and the gospel under the tutelage of the Holy Spirit.

He penned these lines to Titus in reference to bishops (pastors and elders, no doubt):

> Holding fast the faithful word as he hath been taught, that he may be able by sound doctrine both to exhort and to convince the gainsayers (Titus 1:9).

Peter was likewise concerned:

> There were false prophets also among the people, even as there shall be false teachers among you, who privily shall bring in damnable heresies, even denying the Lord that bought them, and bring upon themselves swift destruction. And many shall follow their pernicious ways; by reason of whom the way of truth shall be evil spoken of (2 Peter 2:1-2).

So What's the Answer?

What can we do to prevent the spread of false teaching both inside and outside of the church?

First, we need to align ourselves with churches that believe and teach the fundamentals of the faith—the virgin birth, the God-man Jesus Christ, the inerrancy of the Scriptures, salvation by grace through faith (Ephesians 2:8-9) appropriated through the blood of Jesus Christ (Ephesians 1:7), plus nothing, minus nothing; Jesus' signs, and wonders, and miracles; His death on the cross, His burial, and His resurrection on the third day; and His ascension to the Father and His coming again.

Second, we are to thoroughly check out and examine those who would be our pastors and church staff members. Do they believe all of the Word of God? Are they committed to the Lord Jesus Christ? Is their number-one aim to please and serve Him? Do they sincerely want to reach souls for Christ?

When it comes to selecting church leaders, we must rely on the guidance of the Holy Spirit and quit depending on the externals. We know all too well that the children of Israel chose Saul to become their king based on his appearance and stature. He was a handsome man, but when it came to spiritual leadership and matters of the heart, he was greatly lacking.

Third, we are to teach the Word of God so thoroughly that it builds a wall of spiritual protection around believers and keeps them from false doctrine. To the believer there is nothing like the assurance that God loves him or her. And how can a person know of God's love? Through the Scriptures, which proclaim time and again God's love for His own.

What's more, it's only by constant exposure to the Bible that we develop the ability to tell the true from the false. When we let God's truth permeate every part of us, we get to the point where we can immediately recognize that which is false.

So, both God's love and His Word can provide us with the confidence and the protection we need in order to deflect the influence of false teaching. Do you know the depths of God's love for you? Do you make His Word an everyday part of your life? You can, by devoting yourself to reading, studying, memorizing, sharing, and abiding by God's Word.

Fourth, our witness should be so dynamic and vivacious, empowered by the Holy Spirit, that it will overcome the immorality and false doctrines that are running rampant in our world. No one can win a spiritual "soul debate" when pitted against the pure, untarnished love of Jesus Christ. In a society that is seeing more and more flagrant expressions of hatred between ethnic groups and races, there is nothing more attractive than the love of Christ flowing out from the heart of a believer. God's love is powerful and contagious, but the world won't know about it unless they see it in our lives.

Fifth, we should support Christian colleges and seminaries that teach sound doctrine. If your church, either through special gifts or its regular budget, helps fund institutions of learning, find out which ones. Even if you think they are as solid as a rock, it would not hurt to check them out.

Ask questions. If you can, visit those colleges or seminaries. If their professors have published books—and most institutions insist that their professors do this—make an effort to read their works. Talk with a sampling of the school's students. And by all means help encourage the young people of your church to attend institutions of higher learning that are rooted and grounded in sound doctrine.

Above all, we must expound Jesus in all of His grandeur and glory. Jesus must become personal to all of our hearers, so much so that they are drawn to His irresistible love and incredible greatness. They must be so utterly enamored with Him that there is no room for errant, antibiblical beliefs and behavior.

The number-one strategy for emphasizing the distinctiveness of Jesus Christ is to trust Him, preach Him, teach Him, and live Him. Many people want to debate about Jesus. However, we are called on to delineate Him, not to debate about Him.

If I were called on to debate someone like Madelyn Murray O'Hair, I would simply stand up and say, "I have one sentence for you: 'The fool hath said in his heart, There is no God' [Psalm 14:1 KJV]. That is the conclusion of my argument." Then I would sit down.

While many Christians actively witness for Jesus, there are many who do not. To them I say this: All of the human arguments and writings in the world will not persuade the unsaved one iota unless we allow the Holy Spirit to move through us and on other people's hearts and minds.

An Incredible Privilege

God has called on us human beings to convey His message and share the glowing good news. That is a central function of our ministry—to glorify, magnify, and praise Him to the extent that He stands out. How does He do it? Through us. If we do not speak out for our distinguished Savior, who will?

As Christians, we have no greater privilege before us, no greater calling. When it comes to entering the heavenly realm, there is only one thing we can take with us: the people whom we've reached for Christ. That's what really counts, what really matters. Is that the focus of your life today?

— 8 —

A Worship
Without Spirit

Lyman Beecher Stowe in Saints, Sinners and
Beechers *told that on one occasion Thomas K.
Beecher substituted for his famous brother,
Henry Ward Beecher, at Plymouth Church,
Brooklyn. Many of the people who had come to
hear Henry became restless when Thomas
appeared in the pulpit. Some people started for
the door. Thomas raised his voice and said: "All
those who came here this morning to worship
Henry Ward Beecher may now withdraw from
the church. All who came to worship God may
remain.*[1]

As we approach the twenty-first century, there is tremendous confusion throughout the Christian community on
the subject of worship. Just ask a sampling of church members or inquirers this question: "What is worship?" The
wide variety of answers you get may well astound you; in
fact, you might not get any two answers that are the same!

Many people will reply, "Worship is going to church."
Or, "Worship is singing and a sermon." "Uh, worship is getting together in the name of God." And some of them will

117

immediately snap back, "Well, I don't believe you have to go to church to worship. I can worship just as well while I'm fishing or playing golf—you know, being out in God's nature." But all of those answers fall woefully short of what true worship is.

As we continue through this chapter, I'm going to endeavor to answer the following questions:

- What is worship?
- What is *acceptable* worship?
- What pleases God?
- What benefits the believer?
- What are the elements of worship?

THE BIBLE: A TEXTBOOK FOR WORSHIP

There is no sense in discussing worship without first going to the New Testament and rediscovering the genuine intent and meaning of worship. The *Master Study Bible* defines worship as:

> Respect shown to an object, especially to God; only in a rather figurative sense to beings other than divine (Psalm 45:11; 99:9; Isaiah 27:13; Matthew 14:33; 15:25; Revelation 14:7). The ancient commandment forbade the worship of any but the true God (Exodus 20:3; 34:14). Idols were not to be worshiped nor images made to represent the Lord (Yahweh) (Exodus 20:5). Worship was adoration (Psalm 95:6), praise (Psalm 99:5) and prayer (Daniel 6:11).[2]

R. T. Kendall, minister of London's historic Westminster Chapel, wrote this in his extraordinary book on worship, *Before the Throne:*

Two Greek words in the New Testament are translated by our word "worship." One is *proskuneo*, which is used 60 times and means "to adore," "to give reverence to." This refers to the condition of the heart. It is the word used by Jesus when He said to the woman of Samaria, "God is a Spirit: and they that worship him must worship him in spirit and in truth" (John 5:24). The other word is *latreunos*, which appears as a noun or verb 26 times, and may be translated as "service." This is the word used to refer to public worship, and comes in Philippians 3:3: ". . . who *serve* (worship) God in the spirit." Thus both words are used in the context of Spirit-led and Spirit-controlled worship.[3]

VARIATIONS IN WORSHIP STYLES

At this point there are decided differences of opinion. Kendall feels that true worship must always lead to the proclamation of the Word. There are those who would claim that worship may or may not encompass preaching. They would also contend that worship may be either corporate ("where two or three are gathered together in my name, there am I in the midst of them"—Matthew 18:20), or individual, as evidenced by Isaiah's encounter with God in the temple, when he saw the Lord "sitting upon a throne, high and lifted up" (Isaiah 6:1), and cried out, "Woe is me! For I am undone; because I am a man of unclean lips, and I dwell in the midst of a people of unclean lips: for mine eyes have seen the King, the LORD of hosts" (Isaiah 6:5).

Kendall continues:

> Here, then, is my own definition of worship: it is the response to, and/or preparation

> for the preached word. I say this not because I am trying to defend the Reformed tradition, or because I want to perpetuate my church's tradition as a preaching center, but because I happen to be convinced that worship, as described in the New Testament, makes preaching central....The object of worship is, of course, the triune God. Look again in Philippians 3:3: "We...worship God in the spirit, and rejoice in Christ Jesus." Worship centers on God, with special attention given to praising God for Jesus—for who He is and what He has done.[4]

There is no uniformity about worship styles or patterns in Christendom. There was a time when so-called mainline denominations, by and large, were rather traditional—a piano and organ as instruments, the singing of hymns, a choir if one could be gathered, a responsive reading once in a while, a Scripture reading, the offering, and a sermon by the pastor or a guest preacher. But in more recent decades, we have seen a wide variety of worship styles crop up in our nation's churches.

Many people, when they choose a church, will take in consideration a church's approach to worship. If we were to go from church to church, we would discover a broad latitude in worship today—from the unstructured, informal type of service where the philosophy is spontaneous creativity to a meticulously planned, formal tack that includes prescribed liturgy (i. e., the doxology every Sunday, the Lord's Prayer, sometimes recitation of a confession of faith, and no room for improvisation).

Music styles range from Baroque—such as Bach and Handel—to what folks used to call Stamps-Baxter (featuring a ragtime or jazz beat with almost danceable syncopation).

Instrumentation varies from *a cappella* (where no pianist or organist is available) to an organ and/or piano and to a full orchestra.

There are churches in which a begowned minister and choir march in to a chant sometimes with an accompaniment of trumpets or bells. The minister will ostentatiously move to the split chancel, where there are two pulpits (based on Catholic worship forms). In that type of church there is no room for flexibility, and the printed bulletin rules the day, even with instructions about when to rise and kneel, and when to respond and not to respond.

Then there are still other churches where the attitude is, "We just let the Spirit move." That's okay *if* the Spirit is allowed to lead, but that kind of "freedom" can open Pandora's box for all kinds of worship atrocities. Some "free-spirited" churches actually end up making testimonies and jazzy music more important than the preaching of the Word, allowing a disproportionate amount of the church service to be focused upon music and time for sharing or praise. Such a style of worship leaves a church spiritually malnourished because the teaching of Scripture, which was given to build us up, isn't given the proper emphasis.

It's no wonder, then, that concerned Christians are asking questions like these:

- What are the correct forms of worship?
- What sort of service pleases God?
- What is best for me as an individual?
- Is there a proper approach to worship?

The late, venerable Herschel Hobbs observed:

> Can we really call it *worship* if it is not followed by *service*? It is a mockery to praise the Lord inside church walls unless we tell others about Him outside those walls![5]

> Satan was standing outside a church building one Sunday morning. Inside, the people were singing, praying, and listening to preaching. A passerby asked Satan if it did not bother Him. With a demonic, sneering laugh he replied negatively. Then he added, "They get that way on Sunday, but they will be all right on Monday. It's just a little habit they've acquired." God save us from such a habit. Our worship is to make a difference in who we are and what we do.[6]

Worship styles have changed through the centuries, and of course will continue to change as we move onward through the twenty-first century. There is nothing wrong with such change; to quote that old expression, the Christian is "geared to the times but anchored to the rock." In one sense, our worship harks back 2,000 years. In another we can be more contemporary in our endeavor to reach the people of today. The key is that our worship and our music remain rooted in the teachings of God's Word.

I know that some people find it hard to accept more contemporary music in the church because they were raised in the traditional patterns of the past. But then we need to remember Paul's testimony: "I am made all things to all men, that I might by all means save some" (1 Corinthians 9:22). But how far should we adapt and change? We need to look to the Holy Spirit to inform us, but we need to make sure that God is the focal point and nothing is done contrary to Scripture.

Years ago, I never would have dreamed about some of the changes that are taking place in our church services today. But rather than write off all the changes taking place, we need to consider which changes might be beneficial, and which might be detrimental. There's more to the matter than musical styles. There are staid Christians who eschew contemporary Christian music—they say that most of the newer music is "worldly." Yet today's classics, written by earlier Christian musicians were at one time contemporary. For example, we have sung "Revive Us Again" for generations, yet those who adapted the song picked up the tune from a drinking ditty that goes back to the nineteenth century, called "Hallelujah, I'm a Bum." There are other songs that came from less-than-Christian backgrounds. While the *content* of our message must never change, the *approach* to conveying that message can change.

BIBLICAL *AND* EFFECTIVE WORSHIP

Many of the most dynamic, fastest-growing churches today are the ones that have been willing to stick their necks out and experiment with different styles of worship. In fact, a number of churches offer both a traditional service and a contemporary service or two for the younger generation. So long as the contemporary is not contrived and artificial, it may well reach people that are otherwise unreachable.

> Many of our traditional ministries will continue, but we will need new ways of presenting them....the message must be presented in terms of people's experience. God's message is eternally the same, but the "old, old story" has to be told in a language that late 20th-century residents understand. We must make the gospel clear, understandable, and applicable to this age. And really, nothing is wrong with making it interesting and appealing. Jesus did, and people loved Him for it.[7]

In my book *Real Revival Preaching*, I wrote about the characteristics of a dynamic church, referring to principles for Spirit-filled worship. One of the main marks of a growing church is a climate of enthusiasm. I pointed out that "the word *enthusiasm* comes from the Greek words *en* and *Theos*, which together literally mean to be 'in God.'... Only the church of Jesus Christ can know true enthusiasm, according to its definition."[8]

> If you find an enthusiastic church, you will find an enthusiastic preacher....Lack of enthusiasm is really inexcusable in church. We need enthusiastic preachers in order to have enthusiastic churches....The preaching should not only be enthusiastic, but the services should be likewise. The music needs to be alive! Too many musicians love music more than they love Jesus. If our desire is to please the music faculty at some music school, then we can please the musicians. But if our desire is to reach people for Jesus, we must please our Father in heaven. There is all the difference in the world.[9]

I further pointed out that we should aim for a relaxed atmosphere. There are some churches that are so formal in their worship that you become afraid to breathe or smile. That only inhibits people. A church should be relaxed enough for the Holy Spirit to do His work in the lives of the people.

When Worship Is Real

Ultimately, though most of our worship takes place in the midst of a church filled with other people, each of us must worship God individually. As the old spiritual "You Gotta Walk That Lonesome Valley" expressed it, "There's nobody there but you and Jesus. You gotta go there by yourself." There is no proxy worship.

Why is it that one person leaves a service and testifies, "My, I really had an experience of worship today!" and yet another grouses, "That wasn't worship to me—I didn't receive a blessing, and I didn't get fed spiritually"?

If a church is a gospel-believing, Bible preaching body where Christ is exalted, and a person comes away without a sense of having worshiped, whose fault is it? If a potential worshiper enters a service with a jaundiced eye and a captious spirit, expecting nothing to happen, then *for him*, nothing will. He will not experience worship "in spirit and in truth" (see John 4:24).

Yet in a church service, the minister and other church leaders are also responsible for instilling a spirit of worship. God-sanctioned worship must always point to Jesus Christ, and the worship leaders bear this awesome responsibility. God never called for ministers or worship leaders to impress a congregation with their talent, wit, or suavity.

In the late 1890s a group of Americans visited London and attended a renowned church on a Sunday morning. The preacher was elegant, polished, and sophisticated, and the Yankee visitors walked away, exclaiming, "What a wonderful sermon!" That night they went to a different church and heard Charles Haddon Spurgeon preach, and they departed, crying out, "What a wonderful Savior!"

Preacher, minister, worship leader, minister of music, instrumentalist, choir member—if you are not intent about centering on Christ, you have not only spiritually cheated yourself but also those who have gathered for worship! Every announcement, every note of music, every spoken word, every aspect of the service should amalgamate to the adoration of Jesus Christ. That doesn't mean that sometimes God cannot use a touch of humor or an unusual dramatic or musical presentation. But every element of the service should honor and glorify God the Father, God the Son, and God the Holy Spirit.

Dr. Hobbs wrote:

> A worship service should include adoration and praise, thanksgiving and confession, prayer and proclamation, commitment and surrender to God's will. Anything that does not contribute to these has no place in such a service. For unless our spirits experience the presence and power of God's Spirit; unless we are strengthened, challenged, and motivated in God's will; unless we depart better people than when we came—we cannot be said truly to have worshiped.[10]

— 9 —

A Church Member Without Conversion

*In contrast to sin as an occasional act (undesir-
able, but unfortunately all too common an experience for us and apostles alike), John talked of
others who have no real faith, whose habitual
practice of sin as a lifestyle continues unchanged.
Modern translations of the New Testament show
that the King James Version of 1 John 3:6-9 con-
trasts believers whose new birth changes them
from the habitual practice of sin, compared with
others in whom no new life change appears.*[1]
—Craig Skinner

During my ministry as a pastor and evangelist I have
received much criticism for preaching that true Christians
not only have change of heart, but a change of life as well.
You can tell a real believer by his or her actions. Those who
attend church yet show no fruit in their lives whatsoever
raise a glaring question mark over their professions of faith.

Over the years, I have had thousands of people come
to me saying that although they joined the church long ago
and were baptized, they had never undergone a real conversion experience. Believe me, it was not easy for them to

publicly admit, "I was wrong. Somehow I thought I was saved back then, but I wasn't. I thank God that the Holy Spirit gave me a wake-up call while I still had time!"

Even a number of pastors have chastised me, saying, "Instead of trying to build up faith, you have tried to tear it down. You're using scare tactics when you speak. Why, even some of our deacons, leaders, and other key people are coming down to make professions of faith. Aren't you carrying this business of true conversion too far?"

A Message of Abiding Comfort

In love I beg to differ. God has called us not only to reach people for conversion, but to encourage church members, as did the apostle Peter, to "make your calling and election sure" (2 Peter 1:10). A mere profession of faith shouldn't lull us into thinking that someone is destined for heaven; we should be on the watchout for those who think they are saved but, in fact, aren't. For us to do less is to sin grievously against the Lord who called us to spread His declarative Word. Ultimately, the emphasis on insisting that people have a "know-so" salvation is one of comfort, consolation, assurance, and everlasting peace. The last thing we want to do is to encourage people to place their trust in the unreal, false euphoria of a supposed conversion experience they never had. Can you imagine anything more frightening than thinking that you're a Christian yet finding out, on judgment day, that your salvation wasn't for real?

There is nothing like the assurance of salvation—knowing beyond the shadow of all doubt that Christ is your Lord and Savior, that your sins are forgiven, that all is right with God, that Christ has gone to prepare a place for you, that you are a child of the King, that you are adopted into His family, and so on. It is no surprise that Paul exclaimed, "Eye hath not seen, nor ear heard, neither have entered into the heart of man, the things which God hath prepared for them that love him" (1 Corinthians 2:9).

CHURCHES WITHOUT POWER

The Causes of the Problem

There are a number of reasons that the churches in our nation have lost their influence, but two primary reasons are these:

> 1. Church members who are actually born again but who, because of weak commitment or lack of spirituality, appear to be no different from the lost around them
> 2. Church members who profess to be believers yet have never honestly accepted Christ as Lord and Savior

In the first group you have people whose lives are such that they inhibit the Holy Spirit's work, and in the second group you have people who aren't even indwelt by the Holy Spirit. Take the Holy Spirit out of the picture, and you diminish the church's ability to reach the world.

Frequently I read magazine or newspaper articles in which a secular columnist asks, in essence, "If America is such a Christian nation, why are most churches powerless? Why don't they do something about it?" In other words, even though these columnists take a critical stance, they seem to expect the church to step in and make a difference—which it should, but seldom does. Yet many of these same commentators will write, "But don't talk to us about these old-fashioned ideas about sin. Why, that's 'right-wing, fundamentalist extremism.'" No, that's simply going back to the bedrock foundations that once made this nation great. As the French author de Tocqueville penned, "When America ceases to to be good, she shall cease to be great." Sadly, I believe we have reached that point.

The Crux of the Matter

We as Christians don't like to face opposition or attacks from the world—that's understandable. However, here in America, most of society is simply *ignoring* the church rather than opposing it. People are ignoring us because we're trying so hard to stay quiet and not upset anyone. In going so, we're actually doing more harm to the cause of Christ—it's when we live as salt and light that people are doing to be attracted to God. Yes, we might face opposition, but it's better that we be persecuted and point people toward heaven than remain quiet and hide God's truth from those who need to hear it.

Ours was once considered a Christian nation, but we are now reaching rock-bottom morally and ethically. The consummate tragedy is that even the majority of church members no longer seem to care about our decline. We can be sure that something is desperately wrong when in many areas of our nation, cults and even Muslim religious groups are growing faster than most Christian denominations. In years gone by the evangelical church had a powerful influence and voice across our land. One of the main reasons juvenile delinquency was not a major problem was because of the preponderance of the two-parent family. Also, up through the 1950s, most families—even those who didn't profess to be Christian—adhered to the basic maxims of Christianity and also the Ten Commandments. Most young people were absolutely afraid even to *think* about disobeying their parents or get involved with drinking and smoking. Many an adult or senior today will readily admit, "The reason I didn't do the kinds of things some kids do today is I feared punishment. I loved my parents, and wanted to obey them." Many of them also learned about wrong behavior patterns from church as they grew up—they learned that the Bible prohibits lying, cheating, stealing, sexual immorality, and so on.

GRAPPLING WITH THE PROBLEM

How can we deal with the problem of churchgoers who think they're saved but aren't? If you dare, start having talks with your inactive members. Why aren't they involved? Might there be reason to encourage such people to examine their lives? So few churches today stay in close touch with their flocks and watch out for those who "drop out of the picture." Even in small churches, the reasoning is as follows: "Brother so-and-so is a strong Christian even though he hasn't attended a service in years." Today, amid lite discipleship, too many pastors and active believers are too scared to ask people—especially new members—about their conversion and how they know it's real.

A Call for Real Christians to Stand Up

Author Gertrude Stein is known for the phrase, "A rose is a rose is a rose." I contend that "A Christian is a Christian is a Christian." A person is either saved or not saved, born again or not born again—there is no middle ground. Jesus could not have articulated this truth any plainer: "He that is not with me is against me; and he that gathereth not with me scattereth abroad" (Matthew 12:30).

It's important for us to recognize that church members who have not become saved through Christ are an oxymoron. For a person to formally declare himself a church member—a part of the body of Christ—yet not be saved is contradictory. He is not actually a member of the true church. His name is simply on an earthly roll, and is not written in the Lamb's book of life in heaven.

As Billy Sunday the evangelist facetiously put it, "Rolling a wheelbarrow into a garage doesn't make it a car any more than joining a church makes a person a Christian."

In the New Testament the word "church" (Gr., *ekklesia*) literally means "the called out ones"—the fellowship and spiritual kinship of all those who belong to God through their acceptance of His only begotten Son, Jesus Christ, as Lord and Savior. The writer of Hebrews speaks about "the general assembly and church of the first-born" (12:23), a reference to the true spiritual body of Christ.

As soon as a person is born again and adopted into God's family he belongs to the true church, the body of Christ, which is comprised of every believer throughout the ages. God intends for the local church to exist as a *koinonia* (an intimate fellowship) of those who already belong to the true church, whose members are recorded in the book of life.

Expect Nothing, Get Nothing

Barney Walker, Sr., a faithful preacher who held to Lordship salvation (the perspective that a truly saved person will show evidence of his faith by his actions), penned these lines:

> The Balaam doctrine taught God's people to live like other people in the world. Why not take the women of Midia, and live like the Midianites? Why maintain moral standards that would curb any lustful desire? Why not eat things sacrificed to idols? The Midianites did and they got along all right! Why not have a good time and live it up?[2]

Walker was right on target. "The counterparts of the doctrine of Balaam today...seem to say, 'It makes no difference to us. Come on and join our church; we don't worry about how you live.' How many churches do you know of that do anything about their members who are murderers, whoremongers, gamblers, liars or practice any other grievous sin?"[3]

THE WARNINGS FROM JESUS

Repeatedly the Lord Jesus warned people about trying to enter the kingdom of heaven except through a firm acceptance of Him. He declared:

> Enter ye in at the strait gate: for wide is the gate, and broad is the way, that leadeth to destruction, and many there be which go in thereat: because strait is the gate, and narrow is the way, which leadeth unto life, and few there be that find it (Matthew 7:13-14).

In one of His parables, our Lord spoke of the wheat and the tares (weeds) growing up side by side until harvest time (the end of the world, "the consummation of the age"), when the reapers (probably angels) will appear to sift the acceptable wheat from the unacceptable weeds—a verdict that is of eternal consequence:

> The servants of the householder came and said unto him, Sir, didst not thou sow good seed in thy field? from whence then hath it tares? He said unto them, An enemy hath done this. The servants said unto him, Wilt thou then that we go and gather them up? But he said, Nay; lest while ye gather up the tares, ye root up also the wheat with them. Let both grow together until the harvest: and in the time of harvest I will say to the reapers, Gather ye together first the tares, and bind them in bundles to burn them: but gather the wheat into my barn (Matthew 13:27-30).

In another parable, our Master spoke of the dragnet that would gather up all kinds of maritime creatures, and then the angels who would separate the righteous fish from the bad:

> The parable of the dragnet indicates that many who are brought into the church, and who we name as duly registered members, will at the last be cast out. It is not a question of whether you have been enclosed with the net of the church; the question after all is, Are you good or bad in it? It isn't a mere matter of separating church people from worldly people, but of separating the saved from the unsaved. Jesus cautioned us against saying, "Lord, Lord," and then failing to do His will. The question is not, Are you in the church, but, Are you in Christ?[4]

EASY BELIEVISM OR REAL FAITH?

Because of the "gospel lite" age in which we live, many church leaders and even lay people do not want to introduce people to the demands of discipleship. They do not want their hearers to know that the Christian life involves sacrifice and obedience. They simply say, "Come forward now. There's nothing involved. Step on down and sign a card. Then we'll baptize you, and you'll be a member of the church."

While salvation itself is totally of God, living the Christian life requires our compliance with God's Word. If we neglect to mention the need for repentance *away* from sin and a turning *toward* God, then we have not given a true call to salvation.

Fewer and fewer churches these days have new-member orientation classes, and very little follow-up is done on the new members to ensure that they joined based on a true profession of faith. Too often, churches will accept someone into membership on the basis of a transfer-of-membership letter or a verbal declaration.

Not only are churches failing to help people be sure of their salvation, but they are also watering down the teaching of God's Word, which inhibits the spiritual growth of those who are true believers. This leaves churches with many poorly equipped Christians who are unprepared to face the fiery darts and arrows of Satan. They think, *Well, I belong to the church now, and everything is going to be okay*—but it's not. They are turned loose without ever being rooted and grounded in the Word. They end up facing a hostile world that is out to discourage them, put them down, and confuse them.

Whether you are a pastor, church leader, or lay person, I pray that you are involved not only in outreach and leading folks into the church, but also in encouraging fellow believers to "grow in grace, and in the knowledge of our Lord and Savior Jesus Christ" (2 Peter 3:18).

Now, I can understand why so many of us are averse to insisting that new members go through an orientation class. We tend to confuse that with catechism and confirmation and special classes people must attend to join certain churches, such as Catholic churches. But I'm not talking about giving instruction in formalities; I'm talking about helping people to be sure about their salvation as well as the essential basics of the faith. Let me ask this: "How much is salvation worth?" According to Jesus, it's worth more than all of the cosmos.

> What shall it profit a man, if he shall gain the whole world, and lose his own soul? Or what shall a man give in exchange for his soul? (Mark 8:36-37).

Not only should we make sure to make counsel available to those who desire to receive Christ, but we should also follow through with them, giving them a packet of helpful materials, visiting them, going back through the plan of salvation with them, stressing the importance of staying close to the Lord for the constant assurance of salvation. To do less is to risk giving a person a false assurance of salvation.

When we hear news about parents abandoning little babies, leaving them on a doorstep, in a hospital corridor, or even in a trash can, we become incensed. But what about those new Christians who need to be discipled until they become spiritually strong enough to become a victorious believer who leads others to Christ and disciples them? Do we have the same kind of concern and passion for them as we do for a newborn baby? We should.

WHY EMPHASIZE
THE ASSURANCE OF SALVATION?

Why should we, from time to time, revisit the theme of the assurance of salvation? Why should we ask pungent questions like, "Do you know you are saved, that you are born again, that you are headed for heaven?" Because God wants us to. If a supposed believer finds himself constantly wondering where he stands with God, then he should inquire of himself, *Did I really repent of my sins and completely receive Christ as my Lord, my Savior, my all in all*?

In my book *Real Christianity* I have a chapter entitled "In Defense of Disturbing," which is based on Acts 14:1-7. In that chapter I asked these questions: Does the church have a right to disturb us? Or, is it more the duty of the church to "leave us be," no matter in what condition it finds us? Is the church nothing but a doting grandparent that holds our hands on just any path we choose to walk? Or, does the church have, inherent in its own purpose, a divine obligation to pull us to other paths with more beneficial designations and safer routes—even if that pull might occasionally be a sharp jerk?[5]

We have a divine imperative not only to disturb an unsaved, hell-bound society, but also to disturb seeming

Christians who show absolutely no signs of being saved. Here I speak to the professing Christian who frequently wonders, *Was I ever saved? If I died right now, where would I go?*

> You'll never have peace in your life— genuine, wholesome peace—until you are first of all disturbed about your lost, wayward condition. Sometimes a preacher comes to town and somebody says, "Oh, I don't like what he preached because he got our people all disturbed." We need more men who will get people disturbed about their lives.[6]

Through the years I have delighted in the tongue-in-cheek satire of the "Eutychus & His Kin" column in *Christianity Today* magazine. In one column I came across this:

> ...No one should ever be made to feel guilty in church. It is a liberated day: Down with sermons that correct us! All people should feel good when they leave church.[7]

That attitude portrays what is happening in Christendom today.

No wonder our churches are teeming with uncommitted Christians and pseudo-believers who have never personally experienced God's saving grace! We are to preach the truth in love, but preaching the truth also means proclaiming what God said about sin, repentance, obedience, and spiritual growth. God cried out to the prophets, in essence, "Spare not!"

Certainly a preacher of the gospel wants to be a winsome witness. He does not want to be perceived as one of the stereotypical, hypocritical preachers often read about

in novels and seen in movies or on television—i.e., Elmer
Gantry, or the self-righteous preacher who ends up committing adultery with the very woman he had inveighed
against and supposedly attempted to reach for Christ, Sadie
Thompson, a well-known prostitute on the island in the
novel *Rain.*

We must be willing to accept the fact that if we preach
or teach the Word with love and divine-kindled passion,
some will love us for it and others will hate us. Those who
receive Christ because of our witness and proclamation
will have a warm spot for us in their hearts. Those who
rebel against us may resent us and our message, but it's
better that we take a chance and make sure that the right
message is proclaimed. We don't want to be guilty of mis-
representing God's Word, or changing what it says.

One satirist aptly expressed it:

> Who am I to stand in the way of social
> progress, especially since it is being pro-
> moted by the twin paragons of government
> and media? So, being one who wishes to
> remain on the cutting edge of societal evo-
> lution, here are a few modest proposals for
> the "Politically Correct Bible." Scratch out
> all those biblical references to blind, lame,
> and leprous people. They shall henceforth
> be non-sighted, specially-disabled, and alter-
> nately skinned. Thus, upon being healed by
> Jesus they became sighted, abled, and
> skinned. Little children in Sunday School
> now can sing of "Zaccheus, the vertically
> challenged man who climbed up in a tree…"
> And don't forget Lazarus, who was "termi-
> nally inconvenienced."

And of course, the word *sin* has got to go. Can you
think of a more offensive human description? How about

"morally challenged"? Or perhaps "non-perfect" people. Adulterers can be referred to a "non-monogamous," and liars, simply "non-honest."[8]

MAKING SURE PEOPLE ARE SURE

So what should we do? Some people will reply, "Look, all we can do is offer the gospel to the people around us. We have no means of judging whether or not they are saved. All we have to go on is what they claim."

I agree. But there is no question that we are called to exhort people to be sure about their salvation. We are to echo the words of the apostle Paul: "Examine yourselves, whether ye be in the faith; prove you own selves" (2 Corinthians 13:5).

Here are some questions we need to ask of ourselves:

1. *Are we sometimes more interested in membership numbers than in true newcomers into the body of Christ?* I myself have had the privilege of baptizing thousands of people in my pastoral ministry. The church staff that worked with me tried their very best to be sure that those making professions of faith were truly saved. I pray they were. We could not fathom their inward being as God can, but we did make sure the emphasis was on assurance of salvation and not numbers. We also asked all new members to attend an orientation class to ensure proper follow-up.

2. *Are we too busy to spend the time that's necessary for soul-winning and follow-up?* There is an old World War II song titled, "It Takes Time." Yes, it does. But what is our earthly time in comparison with all of eternity? John Newton's famous hymn "Amazing Grace" has a line that says, "When we've been there ten thousand years, bright shining as the sun...." Have you ever stopped to think about the fact that in eternity, time will be no more? Eternity is immeasurable, having neither beginning nor ending. Isn't an extra hour today worth investing in a precious soul's eternity?

3. *We must train other committed Christians not only in soul-winning but in follow-up.* A conscientious church, no matter how small or large its membership, will call for lay participation in ministry. God does not expect the pastor to do everything by himself. Tragically, there are megachurches today that have only a handful of earnest helpers in this vital area of ministry. The late Roland Q. Leavell, preacher and seminary president, noted in the late 1950s that 95 percent of church members never win a soul to Jesus Christ. I believe we can safely assume that the figure has gone higher in the decades since!

4. *When people respond to an invitation to receive Christ, make sure that they are assured in their salvation.* If someone says he believes he has received Christ but he's not absolutely sure about his salvation, then take the time to talk with him. Make sure he understands the gospel message clearly, help him to possess assurance, and then accept him into membership with open arms.

5. *Emphasize not only faith and believing, but also* repentance, *the often-missing ingredient in our preaching and teaching.* When Paul wrote to the elders in the church at Ephesus, he said:

> I kept back nothing that was profitable unto you, but have showed you, and have taught you publicly, and from house to house, testifying both to the Jews, and also to the Greeks, *repentance* toward God, and faith toward our Lord Jesus Christ (Acts 20:20-21, emphasis added).

The genuinely vibrant church is populated largely by those who can honestly sing these words from the beloved hymn "Blessed Assurance":

Blessed assurance, Jesus is mine!
Oh, what a foretaste of glory divine!
Heir of salvation, purchase of God,
Born of His Spirit, washed in His blood.
—Fanny J. Crosby

— 10 —

A Preacher
Without Power

*Terrible it is beyond all words for Christ's
preacher to be the wrong kind of man....Often
are we correctly reminded that knowledge is
power, but character is far more so. What a man
is, in himself, counts far more than what he says
with his lips or works with his hands. If the
preacher be lacking in fundamental integrity,
then his life is a ghastly, living lie. The men of the
world will bear with our crochets, as preachers,
if we so live as to convince them that we are true,
genuine, sincere men. Every preacher ought to be
such a sincere and unselfish man that his community would be willing to trust its life into his
hands.*[1]

—John A. Broadus

Every pastor should write these words in his little black
book and underline them three times. His is a serious calling—not one to be taken lightly.

One writer had this to say about being a preacher:

A preacher is called to preach. It is
God's orders. He is ordained to preach—it

143

is his church's wishes. He is educated to preach—his teachers expect it....The gospel pulpit is the preacher's throne.... Paul says the cross is central, essential, dynamic, climactic. His deep-laid purpose was to preach, and to preach the cross, Christ crucified. It was his major joy and glory....It should be the living, flaming ambition of every God-called preacher, his deepest prayer, his most impassioned longing, his daily purpose, and his consistently pushed plan to be a preacher of the glorious gospel; not a lecturer, not a pyrotechnic star-scraper, not a flamboyant elocutionist, not an eloquent after-dinner speaker, but a gospel preacher....[2]

The great preacher W. A. Criswell adds this:

In God's economy, there is no such thing as the delivery of this glorious message of truth without a preacher. In the elective purpose of God His will and work are made known to us through a living personality. This is the essence of preaching and is the first, primary calling of the pastor.... Preaching is the truth of God mediated through a man's voice, life, heart, mind, in fact, his whole being. That is why Spurgeon preached from a "rail," not a pulpit desk. He said a man preached with his whole body and it ought not to be hidden.[3]

PRESSURES ON THE PASTOR

We can be certain that any sincere preacher's desire is to preach with power. However, his efforts to fulfill his main responsibility in the best way possible are often dampened by seemingly incessant calls for his energy and time. In many endeavors a pastor can easily become no more than an errand boy for the church, being manipulated by the congregation as though he were a wooden-headed puppet on a string.

Stuart Briscoe made this observation:

> There are three ways by which a congregation exhibits a degree of pressure upon the pastor. First, there is adulation; second, there is manipulation; and third, there is antagonism. *Adulation*, which swells the head. *Manipulation*, which ties the hands; and *antagonism*, which breaks the heart. Those are the pressures from a congregation.[4]

From these pressures the pastor-preacher-evangelist often becomes downright emotionally and physically tired. Those who write about pastoral ministries call this "burnout." Now, some preachers will say, "Well, I'd rather burn out than rust out." But does God's man have to do either?

It's common for a pastor to lack time with his family, and in many churches it is nearly impossible for him to have any close friends in the church for fear that other members will accuse him of playing favorites.

In most churches the pastor is called on constantly for every conceivable—and inconceivable—purpose: not only for counseling, visitation, weddings, funerals, and pastoral administration, but a thousand and one other matters that could be taken care of by someone else, or even let go of entirely. I'm sure that most modern-day pastors can relate to this doggerel about a harried "undershepherd" being sidetracked from the heart of his ministry:

On Monday, he lunched with a Housing Committee
    With statistics and stew he was filled;
Then he dashed to a tea on "Crime in Our City,"
    And dined with a Church Ladies' Guild.

On Tuesday he went on a Babies' Week Lunch.
    And a tea on "Good Citizenship";
At dinner he talked to the Trade Union bunch,
    (There wasn't a date he dared skip).

On Wednesday he managed two annual dinners,
    One at noon and the other at night;
On Thursday a luncheon on "Bootleg Sinners,"
    And a dinner on "War: Is It Right?"

"World Problems We Face" was his Friday noon date
    (A luncheon-address, as you guessed);
And he wielded a fork while a man from New York
    Spoke that evening on "Social Unrest."

On Saturday noon he fell in a swoon,
    Missed a talk on the youth of our land...
Poor thing, he was through! He never came to,
    But died with a spoon in his hand.[5]

A Constant Dilemma

From Within the Church

Pastors in larger churches are often better protected
from overinvolvement in a constant round of extraneous
church and community events and meetings. By contrast,
the pastor in a smaller church is more vulnerable to incessant requests not only to perform the regular duties of his
pastoral ministry but also to consume considerable time
catering to the likes and dislikes and whims and fancies of
the community's citizens, especially those of his church

members. In many such churches, if he does not respond to a concern or request with glee and gusto, it's very likely someone is going to be upset. It is difficult for the man of God when he must say no to his members' requests.

Pastors frequently find themselves pulled in two directions. They usually want to help people if they possibly can. But to help everyone is impossible. There will be times when he simply must say no. At the same time, he has to be careful that he doesn't say no too often. In fact, saying no to certain kinds of requests or certain numbers of them could even harm his ministry or jeopardize his future with the church. When he answers in the negative, insensitive members may accuse him of being aloof, antisocial, or lazy, even though the pastor may be working his heart out on the most important aspects of his ministry—soul-winning and prospect contacts, visiting the sick and shut-ins, equipping the leaders of the church, and sermon preparation.

You may comment, "Well, that's the way it used to be. Today it's different, and people don't have those kinds of expectations anymore." In reality, the expectations have not changed. In all but the larger churches and mega-churches, the pastor—even though he may have a staff—is usually expected to be on call 24 hours a day, seven days a week, 365 days a year (and 366 during leap year).

Yet if a pastor has a large church and a multiple staff, he may also have corresponding multiple problems. The pastors without a staff often moan, "I wish I had a staff to help me do the work of the ministry." Conversely, some of those who have a staff may find themselves saying "Some days I wish I didn't have a staff. There are so many interpersonal hassles." More than we realize, a good number of pastors have to leave their churches because of difficulty with the staff.

Ray Stedman, in a treatment dealing with congregational manipulation, said this:

...then there is the force of manipulation—a tendency to control. Every pastor is subject to it. Today especially, as I travel across the country and in other countries of the world, I am meeting a lot of young men who have begun their ministry in great expectation of accomplishment in the name of the Lord. They are eager of heart and ready to throw themselves completely into a ministry. Time after time I have met with them just a few years after they have taken a pastorate in a church. As we have met, I have found them discouraged and disillusioned. Many of them were on the verge of resigning from the ministry and taking a secular job and forgetting about the call to the full-time ministry they once felt so strongly.[6]

Why is this the case? Stedman replies, "Because they ran up against a tough, hardheaded, unyielding power structure in their churches that refused to listen to the Word of God."[7]

From Outside the Church

In addition to pressures from the congregation, there are constant temptations from within and without. I believe our own Lord and Savior, Jesus Christ, faced every conceivable temptation and yet overcame them through divine power. Why did He, the perfect God-man, have to put up with the devil's nonsense? One of the main reasons was to set an example and encourage us in our constant warfare with the devil:

Since He Himself was tempted in that which He has suffered, He is able to come to the aid of those who are tempted (Hebrews 2:18 NASB).

> We do not have a high priest who cannot sympathize with our weaknesses, but One who has been tempted in all things as we are, yet is without sin (Hebrews 4:15 NASB).

> You have been called for this purpose, since Christ also suffered for you, leaving you an example for you to follow in His steps, who committed no sin, nor was any deceit found in His mouth (1 Peter 2:21-22 NASB).

No matter how severe the temptation, God promises us a way of escape from all that Satan and his demons throw at us:

> No temptation has overtaken you but such as is common to man; and God is faithful, who will not allow you to be tempted beyond what you are able, but with the temptation will provide the way of escape also, that you may be able to endure it (1 Corinthians 10:13 NASB).

While the majority of God's called leaders live clean, upright lives, from time to time we will hear of those who succumbed to Satan's lures. Satan loves to bring a pastor to ruin because he knows it wreaks havoc in the church. When he can trip up a pastor, he can trip up many other people as well. That's why it's so essential for pastors to be diligent about remaining true to their calling and living a holy life. That's the subject of 1 Timothy, a book in which Paul counsels Timothy to be a strong and faithful leader.

WISE COUNSEL FROM A WISE LEADER

Biblical Qualifications of a Church Leader

The book of 1 Timothy was written by Paul to his "son in the ministry," Timothy. In chapter 3, Paul gives some admonitions concerning pastors (bishops, overseers). He says that a pastor must have these qualities:

> [He must be] above reproach, the husband of one wife, temperate, prudent, respectable, hospitable, able to teach, not addicted to wine or pugnacious [volatile, with a "chip on his shoulder"], gentle, uncontentious, free from the love of money. He must be one who manages his own household well...and not a new convert...and he must have a good reputation with those outside the church, so he may not fall into reproach and the snare of the devil (verses 2-7 NASB).

Remain Self-controlled and Godly

In the next chapter, Paul tells Timothy:

> Discipline yourself for the purpose of godliness; for bodily discipline is only of little profit, but godliness is profitable for all things, since it holds promise for the present life and also for the life to come (1 Timothy 4:7-8 NASB).

Be An Example

In the same chapter, the apostle continued: "Don't let anybody look down on your youthfulness, but rather in what you say, how you live, in your love, faith, and purity, be an example to the believers" (4:12, author's paraphrase).

Exercise Your Spiritual Gift(s)

Paul further encouraged Timothy to read the Scriptures publicly, to exhort (preach with conviction), and teach (1 Timothy 4:13). And he cautioned Timothy not to neglect his spiritual gift within (verse 14, see also 2 Timothy 1:6). I like what Paul said in verse 15: "Take pains with these things; be absorbed in them, so that your progress may be evident to all" (NASB). In verse 16 he advises Timothy to keep an eye on himself and on his teaching—and to "keep on keeping on," or persevere.

Abstain from Wickedness

Paul warned Timothy about the need for living an upright, holy life. A man who defiles himself in the world's ways is unfit for use by God:

> Nevertheless, the firm foundation of God stands, having this seal, "The Lord knows those who are His," and, "Let everyone who names the name of the Lord abstain from wickedness."...Therefore, if a man cleanses himself from these things, he will be a vessel for honor, sanctified, useful to the Master, prepared for every good work (2 Timothy 2:19,21).

Run from Sexual Sin

Every preacher, young and old, should heed Paul's firm admonition to Timothy:

> Now flee from youthful lusts, and pursue righteousness, faith, love and peace, with those who call on the Lord from a pure heart (2 Timothy 2:22).

The wise apostle didn't suggest, "Now, Timothy, you're young and living in a secular, worldly society. As a man of

God you may hang around the fleshpots of the world. You're strong, so when the situation becomes conducive to temptation, dear brother, you simply walk away from it." Oh, no. Paul was downright emphatic: "Flee!" Run from those lusts, even as Joseph sprinted away from Potiphar's wife, leaving her clutching his garment in her hand (see Genesis 39:11-12).

Why was Paul so adamant on the point of sexual purity? He was aware of just how powerful sexual temptation can be, for this was a problem in his day as well.

Sexual immorality has probably destroyed more ministries than all other sins put together and disgraced the cause of Christ incalculably.

Sexual sin diminishes and drains a man's power with God as perhaps nothing else can. How's your power with Him? Maybe you have not physically committed adultery or fornication. Yet there is also the arena of your mind. Is your mind a sanctuary or a sewer? How well we remember the words of Jesus—that whoever looks on a woman with lust in his heart has already committed adultery with her (Matthew 5:27-28).

The man of God must gird up against the insidious temptation of sexual sin. In my counseling I have discovered that preachers and their wives sometimes tend to lose their sexual attraction toward each other for various reasons—disagreements, tiredness, and sundry tensions from church and home life and pastoral duties. Then they may begin to drift apart sexually—and then from other standpoints as well.

What are the warning signs a leader must watch for? Pressure. Strain. Tension. Marital discord. General dissatisfaction with one's life and ministry. Lack of prayer, meditation, Bible study, and concern for the lost. Preoccupation with side issues not central to the gospel ministry. These make a man vulnerable to temptation. Sometimes a woman will come along who entices him; other times it may be him who initiates the dalliance. No matter who is responsible for initiating the contact, a pastor (and his staff) need to work hard to set up protective hedges that will eliminate the likelihood of failure in this area.

Strong Men Rendered Weak

David

David is a prime example of "a man after God's own heart" who engaged in willful sexual sin. He lusted, committed adultery, lied, cheated, had Bathsheba's husband killed in the front lines of battle, and sired Bathsheba's baby, who died (see 2 Samuel 11:2-5,6-17,26,27). Even though God forgave David, it is doubtful that he and the kingdom of Israel were ever the same again. Family troubles plagued him the rest of his days, including the rebellion of his own son, Absalom (see 2 Samuel 14:21–19:7).

When a man of God engages in sexual immorality, he seriously grieves the Holy Spirit (see Ephesians 4:30) and "quenches" Him, as it were, dousing His fire with our sins (see 1 Thessalonians 5:19). During the Old Testament era, God would send His Holy Spirit on His servants upon certain occasions for specific purposes—the Spirit didn't permanently indwell those servants as He does New Testament believers today. David evidently was afraid that God might remove His Spirit from David's life, for after his heinous sins, David pled, "Do not cast me away from Thy presence, and do not take Thy Holy Spirit from me" (Psalm 51:11 NASB).

Samson

I wrote about Samson in my book *Real Evangelistic Preaching*:

> But wait! What happened to him? One prostitute, one harlot, one lie to God, and

pretty soon the strong man became weak. A man of God became a man of sin. A holy man became an unholy man. Why did the difference come? The difference came because sin entered the picture....

Here was a man who could destroy a corn patch with fire, but he couldn't put out the fire of lust in his own soul. Here was a man who could break the physical fetters that were wrapped around him, but he couldn't break the shackles of sin that were making his own immoral thoughts captive. Oh, Samson. Didn't you know that sin leads to suffering? They took him. They bound him. They blinded him. Then they put him at the mill to grind like an ox. How true it is that sin binds, and blinds, and grinds.[8]

Eventually when Samson's physical power returned, he used it to destroy himself and the Philistines in the temple of Dagon, their false god.

The Complications of Sexual Sin

Some pastors who allow themselves to become vulnerable can eventually get to the point where they feel that their immoral thoughts or actions are justifiable—they begin to think that their sin is all right because surely they are God's man and are due sexual favors. Such twisted thinking, spurred on by the adversary, the devil himself, ultimately leads to disaster. Even if the man is never found out, there will still be consequences. If he is truly God's man, his conscience will haunt him the rest of his days. There is every reason to believe that David, for instance, seldom rested after his compounded sins against God and mankind. There is disgrace and the draining of power. A man may be forgiven, but that does not mean he will be restored to his former place of influence for Christ.

It pains me how readily so many men have disgraced the high calling of God. A few may recover and to some extent remain involved in some ministry capacity, but they will usually admit, "It's never been quite the same."

The Temptation of Material Gain

Sexual immorality isn't the only trap that can snare a pastor. Another type of love—the love of money and things—is dangerous as well. Those who develop this love often do so because they never had money when they were growing up. It's quite common for pastoral candidates in college and seminary to live in substandard housing and barely be able to eke out a living. No statistics are available, but it appears that the majority of pastors come from middle-class or low-middle-class families, and a few even from abject poverty. As their ministry expands and they widen their circles of influence, money is sometimes thrust before them and they find themselves tempted. In certain churches, too, there is sometimes the tendency for the pastor or other leaders to think, *This is my church, and I deserve whatever I can get.*

The apostle Paul had some stern words about this area of a church leader's life as well. In 1 Timothy 3:3, he said an overseer is to be "free from the love of money" (NASB). Yes, "the laborer is worthy of his wages" (Luke 10:7 NASB). But an inordinate desire for money and possessions will douse the power of the Holy Spirit.

A poet wrote these words about gold, which represents money or wealth throughout the world:

> Dug from the mountainside, washed
>   from the glen,
> Servant am I or master of men.
> Steal me, I curse you;
> Earn me, I bless you;
> Grasp me and hoard me, a fiend shall
>   possess you.

> Live for me, die for me,
> Covet me, take me,
> Angel or devil, I am what you make me.
> —Author Unknown

As an evangelist I am sometimes embarrassed by the money-raising gimmicks and ploys used by certain evangelists and media preachers. The crooked ones are few and far between, but when they are found out, they put Christ and His cause to an open shame. When a genuine servant of God—or even a counterfeit one—flagrantly sins, it causes the enemies of the Lord to curse God and to turn away from Him even more vehemently.

The Snare of Pride

Yet another area in which a pastor needs to exercise care—his view of himself. He must take care that he does not become prideful, calling undue attention to his personality and thus *deflecting*, instead of *reflecting*, the Light of the world. There is a difference between having your personality gleam for God and shining on your own.

We are living in the heyday of pop psychology and New Age notions, both of which ultimately subscribe to the first lie of Satan in Eden: "Ye shall be as gods, knowing good and evil" (Genesis 3:5). In fact, some New Agers teach that they are gods. It's self-esteem this and self-image that— love yourself, promote yourself.

Now Jesus did say that we are to love our neighbor as we love ourselves (Matthew 19:19). Yet He did not mean for us to adulate and worship ourselves. That is mankind's overriding problem, articulated by humanism's view that "man is the measure."

Because of a church leader's position in a church, he can easily begin to think that he is better than everyone else. He may think that because he knows more and he has been blessed with a visible position of ministry, he is something special. He may feel that his opinions carry more weight and are more important, and that he is deserving of privileged treatment. All such thoughts will only lead him higher and higher on the path of pride, which can lead him to a great fall.

The apostle Paul exhorted against pride, calling us to be humble. I like the King James rendering of Ephesians 5:15: "See then that ye walk circumspectly, not as fools, but as wise." Paul also challenged us to look all around us, realizing that not only is the world watching but the heavenly host as well (see Hebrew 12:1-2). And in Romans 12:3 he stated this:

> I say, through the grace given unto me, to every man that is among you, not to think of himself more highly than he ought to think; but to think soberly, according as God hath dealt to every man the measure of faith.

Charles Jefferson, in 1912, made this observation in a book entitled *The Minister As Shepherd*:

> A little Protestant despot, a petty parochial pope, is a sorry caricature of a minister of Jesus Christ. A minister who boasts under his breath that he proposes to run things and who chuckles at his adeptness in manipulating people, and who says by his manner that he is the boss of the parish, is a man who is a stumbling-block in the way of Christian progress.[9]

Unless a preacher is careful, instead of being Christo-centric he will become egocentric. It can happen to any of us if we do not maintain an intimate relationship with our Lord. Before we know it we can find ourselves drifting from close fellowship with Him and relying on our puny selves. As George Duffield, Jr., lyricized in "Stand Up, Stand Up for Jesus": "The arm of flesh will fail you, ye dare not trust your own." Before long we will become aware that God's power has fled from us and, as Christian soldiers, that we are going forth to war with a butter knife instead of "the sword of the Spirit" and are futilely attempting to defeat the devil with a peashooter.

Pray that you will never succumb to pride!

WHEN THE POWER IS GONE

Whether it be sexual immorality, materialism, pride, or some other vice, sin in a pastor's life will drain him of spiritual power. As a vessel of God's work, he has allowed sin to block the "channel of access" that God uses to reach His people. A minister who has indulged in sin is like a clogged waterway that diverts the flow of fresh water to his people. In this way, he becomes one without power—one whom the Lord cannot use in mighty ways.

Now, when a pastor appears to have lost his power, it won't always be because of sin. Remember, there are many causes—some of them related to the staff or congregation, not the pastor. So we cannot be quick to draw conclusions. Rather, we must approach the matter humbly and in prayer, asking that God intervene in the situation and not man.

What is the solution when a minister seems to have lost his power? Humility and neediness are the answer:

> Humility constantly admits, "I can't meet my own needs." Humility falls on its face before God and cries, "My needs will never be met unless You, the living God, meet them."...Humility looks to God to meet its needs....Humility confesses, "God, only You can meet my needs, no one else, nothing

else." When we begin to believe that only God can meet our needs, we will watch God meet our needs.[10]

THE RESURGENCE OF POWER

If ever there was a powerless preacher, it was Peter on the Thursday night and Friday morning of Passover week, when he resorted to violence in defense of his Lord, cutting off the ear of the high priest's servant. Then what did our bold, swaggering "hero" do? Under the cloak of anonymity he slinked around on the dark outer fringes of the trials where his Lord was being grossly afflicted and falsely tried. As Peter waited to see what would happen, he was accused of being one of Jesus' followers. After the third accusation, Peter

> ...began to curse and swear, saying, I know not this man [Jesus] of whom ye speak. And the second time the cock crew. And Peter called to mind the word that Jesus said unto him, Before the cock crow twice, thou shalt deny me thrice. And when he thought thereon, he wept (Mark 14:71-72).

How ashamed Peter must have been! He had told boldfaced lies, denying his own Lord, no less. Yet it was this same man who only 50 days later boldly and powerfully preached to a large crowd, bringing 3,000 souls to Christ! Note what he says:

> Men of Israel, listen to these words: Jesus the Nazarene, a man attested to you by God with miracles and wonders and signs which God performed through Him in your midst, just as you yourselves know—this Man, delivered up by the predetermined

> plan and foreknowledge of God, you nailed
> to a cross by the hands of godless men and
> put Him to death. And God raised Him up
> again, putting an end to the agony of death,
> since it was impossible for Him to be held
> in its power (Acts 2:22-24 NASB).

What was the difference? The resurrection of the Lord Jesus Christ and the coming of the Holy Spirit upon all believers, including Peter!

The solution to a preacher without power is found in the life of Peter. God the Son is alive and lives within us through God the Holy Spirit, our source for power. If one is a true preacher of the gospel but feels powerless, let him call upon God for a recharge, a fresh filling, even as Peter, John, and other believers did only a few days after Pentecost.

> When they had prayed, the place where
> they gathered was shaken, and they were all
> filled with the Holy Spirit, and began to
> speak the word of God with boldness (Acts
> 4:31 NASB).

What happened? I believe we can rightly conclude that these men, who had nowhere to go upon Jesus' ascension into heaven, found themselves in a place of total dependence upon God.

And that's where God wants His called leaders to be: in a place of total dependence upon Him. It's interesting to note that most pastors, when they began their ministries, were in a place of wholehearted dependence because they had no other option. They looked to God to provide their education, their sustenance, and a ministry position. With the passage of time and the experience of success, it's easy to lose that sense of dependence—to look to self, the church staff, and to others to keep the ministry running.

But none of it would be possible without God's power and blessing.

So we who are leaders need to ask ourselves if we are leaning in total dependence upon the Lord. We need to return to the humility that marked our earlier days in ministry. And those of us who are in support roles—the staff and the congregation—need to do all that we can to help our pastor maintain his dependence on the Lord. This can be done through prayer, encouragement, and allowing our pastor time for nourishing his own relationship with God.

— 11 —

A Society Without a Conscience

• *One out of every four children now live in single-parent homes. The ratio will increase to one in two before this group graduates from high school.*
• *At least 20 million people live alone.*
• *In the past 30 years, the suicide rate has tripled. Suicide is the third largest killer of teenagers.*
• *One in three girls and one in four boys are sexually abused by the age of 18.*
• Newsweek *magazine reported that incest perhaps touches one in five Americans.*
• *We have at least 20 million alcoholics in the United States and at least 20 million adult children of alcoholics. Alcoholism affects 128 million American family members, one-half of the nation's population.*
• *Baby boomers are ten times more likely to be depressed than their parents. They are five times more likely to divorce than their parents.*
• *Forty to 89 million Americans suffer from compulsive overeating. Five to 15 percent die from the disorder. At least $20 billion is spent annually by Americans to lose weight.*

> • *Reports of sexual abuse have increased from 6,000 in 1976 to 200,000 in 1988 [author's note: and inestimably more today]. Sociologists claim the problem is far greater than the cases reported.*
> • *In spite of threatening diseases, sexual addiction is on the increase. Those addicted now face the strong possibility of AIDS, which is always fatal. AIDS deaths have skyrocketed.*
> • *Estimates place at least 179,000 persons in emergency shelters for the homeless. The estimated number of homeless in the United States ranges from a low of 500,000 to a high of 3,000,000.*
> • *In the United States 33.6 million live in poverty. That is 13.5 percent of the population, and estimates say that 23 percent of all preschoolers live in poverty.*
> • *The population in state and federal prisons is nearing one million inmates. It is estimated that one out of every two American families is affected directly by crime.*[1]
>
> —James T. Draper, Jr.

That shocking litany, horrendous as it sounds, barely scratches the surface. With all the talk about how mankind has progressed through history, it would seem that our world should be getting better. We would expect to see a more civilized, well-mannered, caring humanity. But that's not the case. Sin and injustice of every kind is on the increase. Killing, violence, and destruction are rampant as never before.

WHY?

Why is our society seemingly bent on destroying itself? Because, except for the influence of the gospel, it is devoid of a conscience. So that we understand what is meant by

the word *conscience*, let me offer a definition: it is a culti-
vated sense of responsibility and the ability to distinguish
between right and wrong. The *Master Study Bible* defines
conscience as "the sense within us by which we approve or
disapprove of ourselves for having followed or failed to follow a moral standard known to us."[2]

Why is America individually and collectively losing its
conscience? It's because of sin—man has chosen to rebel
against God, disobey His leadership and rulings, and depart
from the principles and values designed to preserve society.

Dr. Harold A. Carter, a dynamic African-American pastor from Baltimore, Maryland, published a piercing book
entitled *America, Where Are You Going?* Dr. Carter pointed
out:

> The light that Jesus left His church is
> being dimmed by forces bent on putting
> out that flame. We are forced to raise some
> serious questions as a nation today. Where
> are we going as a people under God? Where
> are we going as a nation? Who is in control?
> Can the accelerating urban decay be ar-
> rested? Can our obsession with a secular
> way of life, bursting over with enticements
> for bodily pleasure, be arrested before we
> drown? What will it take for today's gener-
> ation to read the handwriting of God upon
> our nation's walls?
>
> Instead of the sound of church bells on
> Sunday, we are flooded with the roar of fans
> who fill the nation's stadiums....When the
> season is right, we head to the beach and
> seek the renewal of water and sun. Our
> marathon races for endless charities are fea-
> tured, usually on Sundays, while we retain
> some inklings of faith. Yet, somehow, Amer-
> ica's high percentage of those acknowledging

belief in God...is seldom felt in the arena of everyday life.

When the presence of God is no longer the primary factor in people's lives, the sense of God's wrath and His judgment become mute and meaningless. There is a sense of divine accountability locked up in the question, America, where are you going?[3]

OUR HERITAGE IGNORED

Though secular historians today are trying to rewrite our nation's history, they cannot convincingly deny that the United States of America was established on Christian principles. Our early government documents were based on the underpinnings of the ethics and morals of the Judeo-Christian tradition and are peppered with phrases like "one nation under God," "endowed by their Creator," and "with a firm reliance on the protection of Divine Providence" (all from the Declaration of Independence). The Mayflower Compact, signed by the early settlers of Plymouth, Massachusetts, in 1620, closed with, "In ye name of God. Amen." In Jamestown, Virginia, the first permanent English colony in America (1607) the community leaders acknowledged God in all of their deliberations.

"In God We Trust" is on our coins. And many of the buildings in Washington, D.C. are inscribed with statements about God and passages taken from Scripture.

All this stands as clear evidence of our heritage. But today, society is eager to uproot our nation's Christian moorings. They appeal to what has now become a widely misunderstood concept, the separation of church and state, and assume that it means any expression of Christian convictions or beliefs should be kept private, not public. We are told we should tolerate the expression of all sorts of opinions and worldviews, but society has little or no tolerance for what Christians have to say.

What caused this turnaround? Over the last several decades, Americans have gradually been brainwashed through ungodly influences and have become desensitized to the most outrageous evils and injustices. The Christian psychiatrist, Paul Tournier, summed up our dilemma: "Modern man suffers from repression of conscience."

The Bible plainly declares that a person can fall so deeply into sin and hateful arrogance toward God that he can lose his conscience. We find this affirmed in 1 Timothy 4:1-2:

> Now the Spirit speaketh expressly, that in the latter times some shall depart from the faith, giving heed to seducing spirits, and doctrines of devils; speaking lies in hypocrisy; *having their conscience seared with a hot iron* (emphasis added).

The phrase "seared with a hot iron" speaks of one's conscience reaching the abysmal low of having absolutely no sensitivity—in other words, rendered dead. Peter referred to conscienceless people as "natural brute beasts, made to be taken and destroyed." They "speak evil of things that they understand not," and they "shall utterly perish in their own corruption" (2 Peter 2:12). Frankly, we have an abundance of people today who no longer have a conscience. Often we hear about cold-blooded murderers who express no remorse over their deeds and even admit that they got a thrill out of watching a victim die.

In the face of all this, there are still many people who believe that human beings are essentially good, and have "a spark of divinity." But that's not what we see in the newspapers or hear on the radio or television. We need go no further than the Book of books, God's Word, to see the true state of man's heart:

> Having the understanding darkened, being alienated from the life of God through

the ignorance that is in them, because of the blindness of their heart: who being past feeling have given themselves over unto lasciviousness, to work all uncleanness with greediness (Ephesians 4:18-19).

ACCEPTING RESPONSIBILITY

A conscience that is unresponsive to God is merely an instrument for the devil. He plays on the consciences of unregenerate men and women until their spiritual senses are twisted or non-existent. Those who are devoid of conscience are referred to as having a reprobate (a totally obliterated) mind, a psyche that is set on evil and inconceivable abominations. What's especially tragic is that frequently, people are not held responsible for their sinful actions.

How often have we heard hardened criminals excused from their actions because they were raised in an unloving home, sexually abused, or lived in impoverished conditions? In other words, the wrongdoer is simply a victim of his or her circumstances and cannot help what he or she did. That the criminal justice system accepts this kind of blameshifting is simply one symptom of the perverted and twisted thinking in our society.

What is the major flaw in this kind of reasoning? It doesn't square with what Scripture teaches about man. The Bible makes it clear that we must accept our own responsibility for our actions—we can't blame someone else:

> *Each one of us* shall give account of himself to God (Romans 14:12 NASB, emphasis added).

> All have sinned, and come short of the glory of God (Romans 3:23).

> The wages of sin is death; but the gift of God is eternal life through Jesus Christ our Lord (Romans 6:23).

> The heart is deceitful above all things,
> and desperately wicked: who can know it?
> (Jeremiah 17:9).

> When lust has conceived, it gives birth
> to sin; and when sin is accomplished, it
> brings forth death (James 1:15 NASB).

> There is none righteous, not even one;
> there is none who understands, there is
> none who seeks for God; all have turned
> aside, together they have become useless;
> there is none who does good, there is not
> even one (Romans 3:10-12 NASB).

The problem, then, is not found in a person's outer circumstances, but in his or her heart. Ultimately it comes down to a matter of choice—a matter of how someone chooses to respond to the world around him and the compulsions in his heart. I know many people who had insufferable childhoods yet live upright, responsible lives. There's no reason to say that there's an absolute cause-effect relationship between a person's errant behavior and any perceptions he might have about being a failure or lacking self-esteem.

"Governor Frank Keating of Oklahoma has had it with those who 'naively think criminals are more the product of deficiencies in society,'" wrote Jeffrey Zaslow in his *USA Weekend* column "Straight Talk." Zaslow continued, "He argues that some people are 'irretrievably evil,' and if you want proof, he says, visit Oklahoma. Meet the 500 people injured in the [Oklahoma] bombing, or the 249 children who lost one or both of their parents." [4]

The governor also commented, "You can be sympathetic to the sinner and say, 'Well, he had a bad childhood.' But you can't be sympathetic to the sin. You can't sanction what someone did because of his background." [5]

LESSONS FROM ISRAEL AND JUDAH

God's Old Testament prophets spoke frequently about the characteristics and effects of a society bereft of a conscience. Isaiah wrote:

> Ah sinful nation, a people laden with iniquity, a seed of evildoers, children that are corrupters: they have forsaken the LORD, they have provoked the Holy One of Israel unto anger, they are gone away backward. Why should ye be stricken any more? ye will revolt more and more: the whole head is sick, and the whole heart faint....Your country is desolate, your cities are burned with fire: your land, strangers devour it in your presence, and it is desolate, as overthrown by strangers (Isaiah 1:4-5,7).

Remarkably, much of what Isaiah said about Israel could apply to the United States! It sounds as though he had the United States in mind!

Proclaiming God's stern words, Jeremiah, "the weeping prophet," mourned:

> My people have committed two evils; they have forsaken me the fountain of living waters, and hewed them out cisterns, broken cisterns, that can hold no water (Jeremiah 2:13).

> They are all grievous revolters, walking with slanders: they are brass and iron [symbolic of the coarseness of evil]; they are all corrupters. The bellows are burned, the lead is consumed of the fire; the

founder melteth in vain: for the wicked are not plucked away. Reprobate silver shall men call them, because the LORD hath rejected them (Jeremiah 6:28-30).

Ezekiel the visionary penned these trenchant lines:

These men have set up their idols in their heart, and put the stumbling block of their iniquity before their face (Ezekiel 14:3).

The soul that sinneth, it shall die. The son shall not bear the iniquity of the father, neither shall the father bear the iniquity of the son: the righteousness of the righteous shall be upon him, and the wickedness of the wicked shall be upon him (Ezekiel 18:20).

And Hosea, who forgave and bought back his whoring wife, Gomer, cried out:

Hear the Word of the LORD, ye children of Israel: for the LORD hath a controversy with the inhabitants of the land, because there is no truth, nor mercy, nor knowledge of God in the land. By swearing, and lying, and killing, and stealing, and committing adultery, they break out, and blood toucheth blood (Hosea 4:1-2).

Amos, the herdsman and gatherer of sycamore fruit, railed against the elite and royalty of Israel:

They know not to do right, saith the LORD, who store up violence and robbery in their palaces (Amos 3:10).

Micah prophesied powerfully:

> Ye princes of the house of Israel; Is it not for you to know judgment? Who hate the good, and love the evil (Micah 3:1-2).

Habakkuk decried the rampant injustice:

> The law is slacked, and judgment doth never go forth: for the wicked doth compass about the righteous; therefore wrong judgment proceedeth (Habakkuk 1:4).

Zephaniah warned:

> Woe to her that is filthy and polluted, to the oppressing city! She obeyed not the voice; she received not correction; she trusted not in the LORD; she drew not near to her God. Her princes within her are roaring lions; her judges are evening wolves; they gnaw not the bones till the morrow. Her prophets are light and treacherous persons: her priests have polluted the sanctuary, they have done violence to the law. The just LORD is in the midst thereof; he will not do iniquity: every morning doth he bring his judgment to light, he faileth not; but the unjust knoweth no shame (Zephaniah 3:1-5).

How Should We Respond?

The evidence is all around us: Our nation is losing its conscience. What are we going to do about it? How should we respond?

It has to begin with *you* as an individual. D. L. Moody, the evangelist who was often called "the man who turned two continents toward God," heard a message on becoming "God's man." Although handicapped by shyness and speech impediments, he answered within his heart, *I will be that man!* Until Billy Graham began his ministry, Moody was considered by many the most effective evangelist in modern history. And it began with a determined heart, a firm resolve. So don't say that you can't do anything or that you are powerless. For years I have heard that "the definition of a majority is God...and *you*."

Change must start in your own heart, in your home, in your church—and spread out into your community, your city, your state, and across the length and breadth of this land. Too many followers of our supernatural Lord have acted as though there's nothing that can be done, as if the almighty, sovereign God cannot counter the wickedness all around us. What's more, many Christians have fallen back on the "lite gospel," fearful that if they speak out against sin they will become unacceptable and be considered politically incorrect. Instead of sounding the trumpet of light, we are tooting the piccolos of *lite* religion. Often what's being tooted is not worthy of being called Christianity. We cannot continue to follow the line of least resistance!

Some Christians feel that the only way to bring about change is through the ballot box, voting out those weak of conscience. Yes, we must be active as citizens, but we must also align ourselves with like-minded believers in solid, evangelical movements that oppose our country's being totally dominated by secular humanism. Legislation is good, but far better is reaching people for Jesus Christ.

Our rapidly deteriorating society has been on the offensive, and pushed Christians into a defensive posture. It's time for us to turn the tables. We need to be more zealous about leading lost people to Christ. We need to reflavor our nation with the salt of the earth. Won't you count yourself among those who restoke the fires of evangelism and revival with freshly renewed sparks from the Holy

Spirit? Believe it or not, it's not that complex. You and I as laypersons and church leaders have our work cut out for us, but hasn't that been the case since the inception of Christ's church?

For too long we have thought that the love of Christ somehow means that we cannot forcefully express ourselves—that we cannot afford to offend a soul. The fact is this, however: By our very stand for Christ we are going to upset people anyway. We must remember what Jesus said in John 15:18: "If the world hate you, ye know that it hated me before it hated you." Do not assume that your stand for Christian conscience will be greeted with a pat on the back, whether inside the church or outside it. To the contrary, more than likely it may be a knife in the back.

Our Lord was not merely lecturing when He referred to His followers as the "salt of the earth" and the "light of the world" (see Matthew 5:13-16). With urgency we must sow the gospel seeds that spring up into everlasting life. As we do, one person at a time, we can once again instill a conscience in the people around us. Dr. Harold Carter said it well:

> The good news is that the essential faith of the church remains and will ever remain the same. Nothing can change the truth of God's eternal Word. The bad news, however, is that believers have sacrificed Christian militancy for social and political expediency. All too often the powerful and transforming faith of our Lord Jesus Christ has been lost in the comfort of material things and in affluent lifestyles. The times and conditions we face urgently tell us we must hear and obey with zeal and with passion God's call upon our lives. It is time to return to God. It is time to experience renewal of life through the church.[6]

— 12 —

A Ministry
Without Urgency

A shilling? A pound? Pray what do you say?
Can that be the price of a soul today?
If that were the price you'd be willing to pay,
Come follow these souls on their downward way.
My friend, ask yourself what it's worth to be
saved.
Turn the light of the cross on what you have
craved
Then 'vision the souls now lying enslaved.
You surely will pray and give till they're saved.
—Dean G. Felker

Years ago there was a sitcom in which the star's favorite expression was, "What a revolting development this is!" That may express our sentiments as we feel more and more uncomfortable about conditions in our sin-crazed world— such as the moral decline in our nation and the world at large, the uncertainties about the U.S. economy, the proliferation of crime not only in our cities but even in rural areas, the messy state of health care, the problems with the federal budget, and the debates over how to handle issues such as euthanasia, abortion, drugs, terrorism, and so on.

It's no wonder some people are screaming, "Hey, stop the world—I wanna get off!" Many thousands of them *are* exiting—either by their gradual self-destruction through alcohol, drugs, or sex-related diseases like AIDS, or by instant suicide with the help of a syringe, an overdose, carbon monoxide, a sharp instrument, a gun, or some other means.

A Loss of Influence

As a nation with a Christian heritage, you'd think that Christianity would have a major influence on people in our country. But not anymore. Instead of Christians influencing and reaching the world, we are finding that Muslims, Hindus, and people of other religious persuasions are making converts right in our midst.

For years the churches in my denomination have emphasized sending out missionaries, and I praise God for our world vision. However, all too many of our own members are neglecting their next-door neighbors. Rather than our going to them as we should, now the unsaved from around the globe are coming to us. We Christians have an unparalleled missionary opportunity right at our doors. Yet we are often following the line of least resistance.

Lite American Christianity

American Christianity, for the most part, is blasé and laid-back. Too much is done to try to make people comfortable while they are at church. There is a serious lack of self-sacrifice and commitment for the sake of carrying on the work of ministry.

What's more, churches everywhere are shooting themselves in the foot by getting sidetracked with controversies and peripheral concerns that are almost reminiscent of the Middle Ages "theological" preoccupation with silly arguments such as how many angels can dance on the head of a pin (no joke)! Certain social issues are unquestionably important, but we have allowed ourselves to become pre-occupied with minor concerns while major matters—such as evangelism and equipping the saints—are given lower priority.

REPRESENTING JESUS RIGHTLY

Ultimately, God's purpose for us in this world is to carry on the work Jesus began. He came to save sinners. We are to do likewise, preaching and speaking the Word of God with love—even love for the soul of the abortion doctor, the homosexual, the rapist, the child molester, the atheist, the murderer. Unfortunately, many unbelievers think that Christians who speak out on the moral and ethical issues of the day are bigots and hateful. What doesn't help is that there really are a few Christians who become mean when they attempt to represent Christ, and that puts our loving Lord to an open shame.

Both Love and Justice

In our endeavors to reach a lost world, we are to express the utmost love of the Lord Jesus. The God we represent "is love" (1 John 4:8). Yet, that same God is justice, righteousness, and holiness.

Yes, we should preach positive messages and affirm doing and living the gospel, but at the same time we are called to cry out against the sins and wrongs of our world. Jesus did. Paul did. Peter did. The prophets of the Old Testament did. By and large, all of them were hated by the majority of the populace and lost their lives—only to gain them, of course.

A Message That Seems Foolish

You can be assured that the devil is working overtime in these last days. And he is doing so through individuals, groups of people, and movements, whether organized or unorganized. Certain groups and organizations are laboring with all their twisted might to make Christians the laughingstock of the world. And wasn't that what Paul observed about the essence of the gospel?

> We preach Christ crucified, unto the Jews a stumbling block, and unto the Greeks foolishness; but unto them which are called, both Jews and Greeks, Christ the power of God, and the wisdom of God (1 Corinthians 1:23-24).

To the Jews the gospel of a crucified Lord was a stumbling block (Gk., *scandalon,* from which we derive our English word *scandal*). They were scandalized by the cross. Why, the very idea that humans could obtain salvation through a man who died an ignominious death on a Roman instrument of capital punishment! And then that man was said to have risen from the dead and become alive forevermore!

Likewise the Greeks (a term referring not only to Grecians but also to Gentiles in general) thought of the gospel and the cross as foolishness. In fact, the word translated "foolishness" is derived from the Greek root word *moros,* meaning "dull," "stupid," and "lacking understanding." You already guessed it: That's where we got the term *moron.*

Man Has Not Changed

Unless the hearts of people are changed by the regenerating power of God, should we expect any different response in this decadent age when humanism, agnosticism, and atheism are the gods of the day? The fact is this: the human psych has not altered since sin entered into the Garden of Eden.

You would think that several thousand years of civilization would have mattered, but it has not. Instead of evolution operating in our world, *devolution* has. Instead of becoming better and better, the world has become digressively worse. Jesus, the Old Testament prophets, and the writers of the New Testament prophesied the decline of civilization, indicating that toward the end of time the condition of humankind would become horribly monstrous.

In Bible days there were bows and arrows, slings, swords, battering rams, and the like. Today enough destructive devices exist—invented by so-called evolving, progressive man—to destroy the entire population of planet Earth in a flash. Countries like Iran, Iraq, China, Syria, North Korea, and Libya have stockpiles of nuclear capabilities, deadly gasses, and weapons of germ warfare. Scientists claim that a tablespoon of certain toxic materials now available is lethal enough to decimate an entire metropolis—or even an entire nation—if placed in the water supply or unleashed into the atmosphere!

No, mankind has not evolved to a higher plane of existence. Rather, it has devolved downward on a slippery slope.

WHO WILL SPEAK UP?

Tragically, many Christians today do not have a sense of urgency about our world's demise. They do not feel strongly compelled to reach out to unbelievers in concern over their eternal destiny. We allow ourselves to believe that our work, our climb up the corporate ladder, our acquisition of certain possessions are urgent matters. We put off ministry and evangelism, thinking we'll get around to serving God at a more "convenient" time.

With all of my being I have tried to point out the overpowering urgency of our message. Maybe I shouldn't quote him, but I will. Elvis sang, "It's Now or Never." Christian, it may well be now or never for you. This could be your final day on this earth since God may call you home.

How appalling it is to consider that many thousands of unsaved people will die today without ever having received Christ. They will depart into an indescribably terrifying, Christless eternity. And that's going to continue every single day for as long as Christ has not returned to earth.

We cannot excuse ourselves, trying to squirm out of responsibility and saying, "Well, God is good and just. Since they never heard, God will make a special dispensation for them." Yes, praise God that He is good, kind, and loving, but He is *also* just, which means He will mete out judgment and justice. That's not His heart's desire, for He is "not willing that any should perish, but that all should come to repentance" (2 Peter 3:9). But He cannot ignore people's sins. God will judge people solely on the basis of whether they repented of their sins and received Jesus Christ as their Savior and Lord. The Bible is chillingly plain about this:

> The wrath of God is revealed from heaven against all ungodliness and unrighteousness of men, who hold the truth in unrighteousness; Because that which may be known of God is manifest in them; for God hath showed it unto them. For the invisible things of him from the creation of the world are clearly seen, being understood by the things that are made, even his eternal power and Godhead; so that *they are without excuse* (Romans 1:18-20 emphasis added).

Paul could not have articulated it any plainer: Even the heathen or pagan who has never heard of Christ is *without excuse*. They will have no argument when they stand before the dreadful "great white throne of judgment" (see Revelation 20:11-15). Notice also Paul's point in Romans 1:18-20 that there is enough in nature and in the heavens even for a heathen to recognize there is a Godhead. And what is the Godhead? The Father, Son, and Holy Spirit.

No one—absolutely *no one*—will have the slightest scintilla of an alibi. Where does that leave the "religious" person in the Western world who has heard of Jesus until he is gospel-hardened, as old-time evangelists used to express it?

Every unbeliever, enlightened or unenlightened, will spend eternity in hell. Jesus' parable of the steward and the servants in Luke 12:42-48, however, indicates that just as there will be degrees of reward in heaven (see 1 Corinthians 3:12-15), so there will be degrees of punishment in hell.

You no doubt are familiar with the account. The landowner (the lord) left his property (household) in the charge of his stewards, also called servants (verses 42-43). It is unmistakable that the stewards represent every human being, and the lord stands for God Himself. One can never improve on quoting the text itself:

> The lord of that servant will come in a day when he looketh not for him, and at an hour when he is not aware, and will cut him in sunder, and will appoint him his portion with the unbelievers (verse 46).

Notice what the next verse says:

> And that servant, *which knew his lord's will*, and prepared not himself, neither did according to his will, *shall be beaten with many stripes* (verse 47, emphasis added).

In contrast, note the fate of the unknowing servant:

> *But he that knew not*, and did commit
> things worthy of stripes, *shall be beaten with
> few stripes* (verse 48, emphasis added).

Jesus' hearers were listening to the true message of God—in fact, looking the incarnate truth of God in the face—so they, as "servants," were fully responsible, and their rejection of that message would result in the severest punishment when the lord (Jesus Himself) would return.

> For unto whomsoever much is given, of
> him shall be much required: and to whom
> men have committed much, of him they
> will ask the more (verse 48).

So, those who know the Lord's will and fail to do it will suffer the worst in hell ("many stripes"), whereas those who do not know the Lord's will, according to Jesus, will suffer less in that forsaken place ("few stripes"). That has nothing to do with a person's duration of time in hell. It merely means that some people will suffer more in hell than others. The more light (awareness) a person receives, the more that will be required of him. Yes, there are degrees of punishment in hell, but that should give no Christian who loves lost souls any kind of comfort or solace.

The lost man who goes to church often will have far more to answer for than the non-Christian Asian or African who has seldom, if ever, heard the precious name of Jesus.

Ignorance Is No "Out"

Some believers argue that ignorance will guarantee an escape from judgment and punishment. But that's not true. If an ignorant person could still be saved, then we would be sinning by following through on the Great Commission and carrying the gospel to the uttermost parts of the earth.

Why? Because then we would be exposing them to the truth in Christ, and they no longer would have an alibi that they were ignorant of Him and had never heard the declaration of salvation. Thus, we would be sentencing them to hell by exposing them to the Lord Jesus.

But the awful reality is this: Every responsible person who reaches the age of accountability, the point at which he or she can make a moral and ethical decision for or against Christ, *has no choice but to choose.*

CULTIVATING A SENSE OF URGENCY

The American church has lost its sense of urgency to the extent that an insidious creeping universalism has crawled surreptitiously into our congregations. At one time it was only unsaved people who would say, "A good, loving God isn't going to send anybody to hell," but now we hear that from, of all people, professing Christians!

God warned the prophet Ezekiel:

> So thou, O son of man, I have set thee a watchman unto the house of Israel; therefore thou shalt hear the word at my mouth, and warn them from me. When I say unto the wicked, O wicked man, thou shalt surely die; if thou dost not speak to warn the wicked man from his way, that wicked man shall die in his iniquity; *but his blood will I require at thy hand* (Ezekiel 33:7-8, emphasis added).

God has not changed. Every saved person is automatically commissioned by his or her Savior to be a watchman or watchwoman. We have no option, no choice not to warn the unsaved. You and I as lovers of Jesus are responsible for carrying Christ's message everywhere we go. And we must do it with a flaming, passionate fervor.

Urgency Begins with the Pastor

A Key Priority

If you are a pastor, I can empathize with you. I was in the pastorate for years before entering full-time evangelism. The task of the pastorate seems to become more complex every day. You have the burdens and cares of your people on you. Unfortunately, they sometimes cause you far more grief and trouble than those outside of the church!

A pastor's workload within the church often makes it difficult for him to develop outreach ministries that can make an impact on the surrounding community. If you have a rather small church (really, in God's sight no Holy Spirit-motivated, gospel-preaching, Bible-believing church is small), sometimes you have almost no help at all, unless God has gifted you with a core of mightily dedicated laypersons who will assist in contacts and visitation.

But, no matter what your church situation, your number-one concern must be the lost, not those already in the sheepfold, even though you cannot afford to neglect them either. I would suggest that at least once a week you read the parables of the lost sheep, the lost coin, and the lost son in Luke 15:3-24.

The Latin word for *pastor* means "shepherd" (which is *poimen* in the New Testament Greek). The good pastor-shepherd (Jesus is the good Shepherd with a capital S) must periodically leave the flock already safe in the fold (representative of being in the sheltering protection of salvation) to seek out even that one lost sheep.

If your people are caring and loving, they will understand that your utmost urgency, as well as theirs, is to "seek and to save that which was lost" (Luke 19:10). We seek them, and Jesus, the Shepherd of all shepherds, saves them.

Yes, you are expected to visit the sick, the shut-ins, and the elderly. Pray that God will give you the strength and stamina to do all you should, but there is nothing worse than to neglect those lost, unsaved sheep.

An Effective Role Model

How can you convey the urgency of reaching the lost? You must incorporate it into your lifestyle. It thrilled my heart to hear one pastor of a megachurch with 20,000 members testify, "I have no excuse, in spite of all my responsibilities to lead the staff and administer the work of my church (which also has a number of associate pastors), not to do soul-winning visitation with regularity. As busy as I am I try to make at least ten or more soul-winning visits per week." In addition he will often invite the unsaved to eat lunch "on him." He tries to make every minute count.

O. S. Hawkins, pastor of First Baptist Church, Dallas, zeroed in on pastors:

> Where do we acquire the passion needed in our public appeals? One with discernment can listen to a person issue a public appeal and usually tell in an instant whether that person is a soul-winner. It normally shows in the passion of his voice and countenance. If the preacher is not issuing the appeal personally day by day, it is difficult productively to issue the appeal in the pulpit.[1]

We must convey this urgency to our people. An unconcerned pastor who glibly drips honey from his mouth may get by with it for awhile. But eventually his congregation will think *Well, our pastor's not concerned about the lost. Why should I be?* Now church members shouldn't reason that way, but what can you expect? They ought to care and express concern regardless, but more than likely they will imitate their minister.

A Proper Balance

Now I realize that if you're a pastor, you must have a balanced preaching ministry. You can't (and shouldn't) preach the same kind of sermon every service. You ought to run the gamut of God's glorious, melodious message of redemption, and most of your messages should have relevant content for both the Christians and the lost.

If you preach nothing but evangelistic sermons with appeals to the unsaved, the Christians in your congregation will rejoice that you are preaching for conversions, but they will also leave the service spiritually unfed. If you preach mostly to the Christians, then you might not get much of a response from the unsaved. So once again, you need to work at both reaching the lost and providing spiritual nourishment for those who are growing in their relationship with Christ.

Urgency Continues with the Layperson

Laypersons, the same goes for you. You, too, bear the responsibility of serving as a witness for Christ whenever you can. There is every conceivable place to witness. At work, on the bus, in a carpool, on the street corner, in a restaurant, waiting in a line, at the service station, in stores, in malls, in your neighborhood, you name it. It's amazing how many Christians complain, "Oh, I just don't know anybody that's lost." If they had the sense of urgency I've been talking about in this chapter, their eyes would become opened and they would come to realize just how many unsaved people are around them.

If you will open yourself up to the Holy Spirit, folks will cross your path whom you can talk with about Jesus. Isn't it embarrassing that the sadly misguided Mormons and Jehovah's Witnesses are well-known for their massive witnessing ministries, putting us timid evangelicals to shame?

It's Now or Never

I knew an elderly preacher who used to tell his hearers, "If you're going to do anything for Jesus, you had better do it now." Oh, how true! "Now is the accepted time; behold, now is the day of salvation" (2 Corinthians 6:2). Urgency screams out, "Do it now!" Jesus tells us, "Do My work now. Occupy till I come. Carry out My Great Commission. Let your light so shine that people may see your good works and glorify My Father in heaven."

Urgency means that whatever you are going to do for Jesus you'd better do right now. I'm sure you've had times when you've thought to yourself, *Well, I really ought to share the gospel with so and so, but I'll wait. There'll be time.* Will there be time? You're not thinking about that unsaved person by accident. God the Holy Spirit has placed that person on your heart and mind.

When you feel such an impulse cross your mind, you want to spring into action. I've had times when I've dreamed about a lost person I know. When that happens, I usually wait until the following morning and then contact them as soon as possible.

At one time, many churches would sing songs that spoke of the great need to reach out to the lost. But these kinds of songs seem to have fallen out of favor, and while many of the contemporary songs we sing are honoring to God, they seldom have reference to the urgency of evangelizing the lost.

What about "Rescue the Perishing" by the blind poetess-lyricist Fanny J. Crosby?

> Rescue the perishing, Care for the dying,
> Snatch them in pity from sin and the grave;
> Weep o'er the erring one, Lift up the fallen,
> Tell them of Jesus the mighty to save.

Rescue the perishing, Duty demands it;
Strength for thy labor the Lord will provide;
Back to the narrow way Patiently win them;
Tell the poor wanderer a Savior has died.

Rescue the perishing, Care for the dying;
Jesus is merciful, Jesus will save.

Or Charles Luther's "Must I Go, and Empty-Handed"?

Must I go and empty-handed, Thus my dear
Redeemer meet?
Not one day of service give Him, Lay no tro-
phy at His feet?

O ye saints, arouse, be earnest, Up and work
while yet 'tis day;
Ere the night of death o'er-take thee, Strive
for souls while still you may.

"Must I go, and empty-handed?" Must I meet
my Savior so?
Not one soul with which to greet Him: Must I
empty-handed go?

I wonder why so many of our churches don't want to sing songs like these anymore. There is a heartrending urgency about rescuing the perishing and caring for the dying. Pastor, layperson, how many people will you carry to heaven with you? Will some of you go empty-handed? Now you don't have to worry about losing your salvation or your place as a believer just because you have never won a soul to Jesus, but can you imagine meeting the Lord face to face and thinking, *I am here to live with my Lord throughout eternity, but I didn't bring anybody with me. Not one soul with which to greet Him. I'm empty-handed.*

That is embarrassing and hurtful to contemplate. Vow right this moment that you will express your urgency by relying on the Holy Spirit's power to reach souls for Christ!

That ancient song, "Brethren, We Have Met to Worship" by George Atkins, paints a poignant picture:

> Brethren, see poor sinners round you
> Slumbering on the brink of woe;
> Death is coming, hell is moving,
> Can you bear to let them go?
> See our fathers and our mothers,
> And our children sinking down;
> Brethren, pray, and holy manna
> Will be showered all around.

G. Ernest Thomas spoke of an Englishman from a past generation, Robert Arthington, who gave his all to share the gospel. He lived in one room, cooked his own meals, and helped students who needed help. Though he may have appeared poor, he gave Christian missions more than $25,000,000 during his lifetime. Following his call to his "long home," this note was found on a small piece of paper: "Gladly would I make the floor my bed, and a box my chair, and another box my table rather than that men should perish for want of the knowledge of Christ." Arthington lived out his life heeding the urgency of Christ's cause. How is it with you?

What If...?

What would you think of a crew of firemen who merely stood around and served refreshments while a house burned to the ground? What if two fishermen were in a boat within reach of a drowning person, and instead of rescuing her they cracked jokes about her inability to swim? What if you yourself were one of those firemen, or one of those fishermen?

You might be thinking, *I'd never ignore someone who's in a life-threatening situation!* But look at these hypothetical questions this way: What are you doing to keep people from burning up in the fires of hate and hell? What are you doing while Satan actively continues to poison the hearts and minds of children, young people, and adults, dragging them down into hell with him and his angels? And what are you doing as people are drowning in the cesspool of sin all around us?

It's not enough to simply place a "Welcome" sign outside the church. Turning the church facilities into an entertainment draw won't do it. An emphasis on performances and slick music without any substantive, Spirit-empowered Bible teaching won't do it. None of these things will turn the tide. Besides, unsaved people are very good at detecting insincere efforts to bring them to Christ.

IT'S POSSIBLE, WITH GOD'S HELP

Following through on the urgency of reaching the lost will require that you have that same sense of urgency in your prayers. How long has it been since you kneeled in heartbroken grief over the hearts of men and women, boys and girls? How long has it been since you put feet on your prayers and went to a person and confessed, "Look, I know I haven't been the best Christian you've ever seen, and I've waited too long. But I want to share my Jesus with you. Why? Because I care for you, and above all else, I want you to be saved and to know where you're going, to have peace in your life."

Don't tell me you can't do it. You *can*, with God's power. Maybe you consider yourself an introvert. You may excuse yourself by saying,"I just don't know how to talk to people." God will help you even as He did Moses, who undoubtedly had a speech impediment; even as He put His words into Jeremiah's mouth—the same Jeremiah who protested, "O Lord, I am but a child." God will reply, "I have put My words into your mouth."

I want to ask you. If you don't go, who will? Don't assume that someone else is going to step in to do the soul-winning you are called to do. If you don't go and witness to the people that the Lord lays on your heart, perhaps no one will ever make that contact.

A. J. Gordon wrote:

> I have long since ceased to pray, "Lord, have compassion on a lost world." I remember the day and the hour when I seemed to hear the Lord rebuking me for making such a prayer. He seemed to say to me, "I have had compassion on a lost world, and now it is for you to have compassion!"[2]

It is *your time* for urgency...this moment!

Notes

Chapter 1

1. John F. MacArthur, *The Vanishing Conscience* (Dallas, TX: Word Publishing, 1994), p. 42.
2. George Barna, Barna Research Group, *1993-1994 Report* (Ventura, CA: Regal Books, 1994), p. 82. Used with permission.
3. Ibid., p. 15.
4. Ibid., p. 83.
5. Loraine Boettner, *Studies in Theology*, (Grand Rapids, MI: Eerdmans, 1960), p. 278.
6. Bailey E. Smith, *Nothing But the Blood* (Nashville, TN: Broadman Press, 1987), pp. 182-83.
7. Ibid., pp. 25-29.
8. Ibid., pp. 30-34.
9. Ibid., pp. 34-38.
10. Ibid., pp. 38-42.

Chapter 2

1. Charles Stanley, *Confronting Casual Christianity* (Nashville: Broadman Press, 1985), pp. 52-53.
2. Gerald Cowen, *Salvation: Word Studies from the Greek New Testament* (Nashville: Broadman Press, 1990), p. 76.
3. Ibid., p. 77.
4. W. O. Carver on "Lord" in *The International Standard Bible Encyclopedia* (Grand Rapids: Eerdmans, 1956, reprinted 1978), p. 1919.
5. Walter Thomas Conner, *Christian Doctrine* (Nashville: Broadman Press, 1937), pp. 194-95.
6. *Kurios* in the *Analytical Greek Lexicon* (New York: Harper & Brothers, n.d.), p. 244.
7. Charles Stanley, *Confronting Casual Christianity*, pp. 163-64.
8. Ibid., pp. 164-66.
9. Fred Wolfe, *The Divine Pattern* (Nashville: Broadman Press, 1983), pp. 56-57.

Chapter 3

1. Quoted in *1000 Illustrations for Preaching and Teaching* by G. Curtis Jones (Nashville: Broadman Press, 1986), pp. 154-55.

2. George Barna, Barna Research Group, *1993-1994 Report* (Ventura, CA: Regal Books, 1994), p. 139.
3. John F. MacArthur, Jr., *The Vanishing Conscience* (Dallas: Word Publishing, 1994), p. 107.
4. Leonard Sanderson and Ron Johnson, *Evangelism for All God's People* (Nashville: Broadman Press, 1990), p. 35.
5. Charles H. Spurgeon, *My Sermon Notes* (Westwood, NJ: Revell, n.d.), p. 990.
6. W. A. Criswell, *What to Do Until Jesus Comes Back* (Nashville: Broadman Press, 1975), pp. 51-52.

Chapter 4

1. "The Upside of Pessimism" by Charles Colson in *Christianity Today*, August 15, 1994, p. 64.
2. "The Gospel of God for the Nations" by John A. Mackay in Don M. Aycock, compiler and editor, *Preaching with Purpose and Power* (Macon, GA: Mercer University Press, 1982), pp. 104-5.
3. O. S. Hawkins, *Where Angels Fear to Tread* (Nashville: Broadman Press, 1984), pp. 83-84.
4. Adapted from account given in "Compromise" by J.H. Dampier in *Treasury of Gospel Gems: Timothy Through Revelation*, Theodore W. Engstrom, compiler and editor (Grand Rapids, MI: Zondervan Publishing House, 1949), p. 140.

Chapter 5

1. E. W. Price, Jr., *The Character Connection* (Shippensburg, PA: Destiny Image Publishers, 1991), p. 81.
2. "Undivided heart" by Ramsey Pollard in R. Earl Allen and Joel Gregory, compilers, *Southern Baptist Preaching Yesterday* (Nashville: Broadman Press, 1991), p. 377.
3. Bob W. Brown, *The Church Is People* (Nashville: Broadman Press, 1976).
4. *Christianity Today*, November 14, 1994, p. 31.
5. Charles L. Wallis, editor, *A Treasury of Sermon Illustrations* (Nashville: Abingdon Press, 1950), p. 62.
6. Frances Meeker, *Nashville Banner*, May 1, 1992.
7. Anita Bryant, *A New Day* (Nashville: Broadman Press, 1992), p. 30.

Chapter 6

1. Don J. Gutteridge, Jr., *The Defense Rests Its Case* (Nashville: Broadman Press, 1975), p. 15.
2. W. A. Criswell, *With a Bible in My Hand* (Nashville: Broadman Press, 1978), p. 136.
3. Quoted by David Dockery in *The Doctrine of the Bible* (Nashville: Convention Press, 1992), p. 40; from James Barr, *Fundamentalism* (London: S.C.M. Press Ltd., 1977), p. 78.

4. W.A. Criswell, "The Preservation of the Word of God" in R. Earl Allen and Joel Gregory, compilers, *Southern Baptist Preaching Today* (Nashville: Broadman Press, 1987), p. 51.
5. Dockery, *The Doctrine of the Bible*, p. 45.
6. Ibid., pp. 43-44.
7. Edward P. Blair, *Abingdon Bible Handbook* (Nashville: Abingdon Press, 1975), pp. 379ff.
8. Nelson Glueck, *Rivers in the Desert: A History of Negev* (Philadelphia: Jewish Publications Society of America, 1969), p. 31.
9. Gutteridge, *The Defense Rests Its Case*, pp. 23-24.

Chapter 7

1. George Barna, Barna Research Group, *1993-1994 Report* (Ventura, CA: Regal Books, 1994), p. 83.
2. G. Campbell Morgan, *The Crises of the Christ* (New York: Fleming H. Revell Co., 1936), p. 79.
3. Ray Waddle, *The Tennessean*, December 25, 1994, p. 12-A.
4. Ibid.
5. Ibid.
6. Susan Cyre, "Fallout Escalates Over 'Goddess' Sophia Worship," *Christianity Today*, April 4, 1994, p. 74.
7. Ibid.
8. Ibid.
9. Charles R. Swindoll, *Growing Deep in the Christian Life* (Portland, OR: Multnomah Press, 1986), p. 29.
10. Ibid.

Chapter 8

1. Charles L. Wallis, editor, *A Treasury Of Sermon Illustrations* (Nashville: Abingdon Press, 1950), p. 292.
2. *Master Study Bible*, "Worship" (Nashville: Holman Bible Publishers, 1981), p. 2253.
3. R. T. Kendall, *Before the Throne* (Nashville: Broadman Press, 1993), pp. 15-16.
4. Ibid., pp. 16-17.
5. Herschel H. Hobbs, Ronald K. Brown, compilers, *My Favorite Illustrations* (Nashville: Broadman Press, 1990), p. 272.
6. Ibid., p. 272.
7. James T. Draper, Jr., *Bridges to the Future: A Challenge to Southern Baptists* (Nashville: Broadman Press, 1994), p. 78.
8. Bailey E. Smith, *Real Revival Preaching* (Nashville: Broadman Press, 1982), p. 113.
9. Ibid., p. 114.
10. Hobbs, *My Favorite Illustrations*, p. 272.

Chapter 9

1. Craig Skinner, *Back Where You Belong* (Nashville: Broadman Press, 1980), p. 24.
2. Barney Walker, Sr., *Seven Spiritual Ships* (New York: Exposition Press, Inc., 1959), p. 32.
3. Ibid.
4. Paul E. Holdcraft, *Cyclopedia of Bible Illustrations* (Nashville: Abingdon Press, 1957), p. 346.
5. Bailey E. Smith, *Real Christianity* (Nashville: Broadman Press, 1979), p. 90.
6. Ibid., p. 97.
7. "Eutychus & His Kin: The X-Rated Pulpit," *Christianity Today*, February 17, 1984, p. 8.
8. "PC" from *Illustration Digest*, July/August 1992, p. 14.

Chapter 10

1. John A. Broadus, "Preachers and Preaching," *Follow Thou Me* (Nashville: The Sunday School Board of the Southern Baptist Convention, 1919), p. 64.
2. Lee Rutland Scarborough, *My Conception of the Gospel Ministry* (Nashville: The Sunday School Board of the Southern Baptist Convention, 1935), pp. 56-57.
3. W. A. Criswell, *With a Bible in My Hand* (Nashville: Broadman Press, 1978), p. 25.
4. Stuart Briscoe quoted in "Ministering in the Future Church" by Ray C. Stedman, Ralph W. Neighbour, Jr., compiler, *Future Church* (Nashville: Broadman Press, 1980), pp. 91-92.
5. Author unknown, quoted in W. A. Criswell, *Criswell's Guidebook for Pastors* (Nashville: Broadman Press, 1980), pp. 65-66.
6. Ralph W. Neighbour, Jr., *Future Church*, p. 93.
7. Ibid.
8. Bailey E. Smith, *Real Evangelistic Preaching* (Nashville: Broadman Press 1981), pp. 20-21.
9. Quoted in Neighbour, *Future Church*, p. 90.
10. Fred H. Wolfe, "The Call to Humility," R. Earl Allen and Joel Gregory, compilers, *Southern Baptist Preaching Today* (Nashville: Broadman Press, 1987), p. 454.

Chapter 11

1. James T. Draper, Jr., *Bridges to the Future* (Nashville: Convention Press, 1994), pp. 110-12.
2. "Conscience" in *Master Study Bible* (Nashville: Holman Bible Publishers, 1981), p. 1745.

3. Harold A. Carter, *America, Where Are You Going?* (Baltimore, MD: Gateway Press, 1994), pp. 4-5.
4. Jeffrey Zaslow, "Frank Keating: No excuse for evil," *USA Weekend*, August 4–6, 1995, p. 14.
5. Ibid.
6. Carter, *America, Where Are You Going?*, p. 108.

Chapter 12

1. O. S. Hawkins, *Drawing the Net* (Nashville: Broadman Press, 1993), pp. 48-49.
2. Paul E. Holdcraft, *Cyclopedia of Bible Illustrations* (Nashville: Abingdon Press, 1957), p. 279.

Other Good
Harvest House Reading

BRUCE & STAN'S GUIDE TO GOD
by *Bruce Bickel* and *Stan Jantz*

This fresh, practical guide to the Christian life is designed to both
help new believers get started and recharge the batteries of believers
of all ages. Humorous subtitles, memorable icons, and powerful
learning aids present even difficult concepts in a simple way. Perfect
for personal use or group study.

THE COMPLETE BOOK OF BIBLE ANSWERS
by *Ron Rhodes*

This great resource addresses difficult Bible questions that arise during Bible studies and witnessing, and covers topics that range from
the conflicts between science and the Bible to reconciling God's sovereignty with man's free will.

WHY THE CROSS CAN DO WHAT POLITICS CAN'T
by *Erwin Lutzer*

Christians cannot expect politics or social reform to change people
when the real battle is not political or moral, but spiritual. Instead,
we need to rely on a power that can change people's hearts rather
than their minds. We can find this power in the cross of Christ. How
can we use the cross to "turn the world upside down" as the early
church did? What kinds of changes can we possibly bring about?
This is the message of *Why the Cross Can Do What Politics Can't*.

PATHWAY TO THE HEART OF GOD
by *Terry W. Glaspey*

Classic writings of faith overflow with inspiring thoughts on the wonder and power of communion with God. Weaving these thoughts
together with insightful narrative, Glaspey takes readers on a stirring
journey to God's heart through the discipline and delight of prayer.

THE HEART OF CHRISTIANITY
by *Ron Rhodes*

This book, excellent for believers and seekers alike, explores the major doctrines of Christianity, including how God, man, salvation, the church, angels and the afterlife, relate directly to Christ.

Dear Reader,

We would appreciate hearing from you regarding this Harvest House nonfiction book. It will enable us to continue to give you the best in Christian publishing.

1. What most influenced you to purchase *Taking Back the Gospel?*
   - ❏ Author
   - ❏ Subject matter
   - ❏ Backcover copy
   - ❏ Recommendations
   - ❏ Cover/Title
   - ❏ Other_____

2. Where did you purchase this book?
   - ❏ Christian bookstore
   - ❏ General bookstore
   - ❏ Department store
   - ❏ Grocery store
   - ❏ Other_____

3. Your overall rating of this book?
   - ❏ Excellent   ❏ Very good   ❏ Good   ❏ Fair   ❏ Poor

4. How likely would you be to purchase other books by this author?
   - ❏ Very likely   ❏ Not very likely   ❏ Somewhat likely   ❏ Not at all

5. What types of books most interest you? (Check all that apply.)
   - ❏ Women's Books
   - ❏ Marriage Books
   - ❏ Current Issues
   - ❏ Christian Living
   - ❏ Bible Studies
   - ❏ Fiction
   - ❏ Biographies
   - ❏ Children's Books
   - ❏ Youth Books
   - ❏ Other_____

6. Please check the box next to your age group.
   - ❏ Under 18 ❏ 18-24 ❏ 25-34 ❏ 35-44 ❏ 45-54 ❏ 55 and over

Mail to: Editorial Director
Harvest House Publishers
1075 Arrowsmith
Eugene, OR 97402

Name_____

Address _____

State _____ Zip _____

Thank you for helping us to help you in future publications!